Holt California Social Studies

World History
Medieval to Early
Modern Times

HOLT, RINEHART AND WINSTON

A Harcourt Education Company

Orlando • **Austin** • New York • San Diego • Toronto • London

Contents

Interactive Reader and Study Guide

Contents

Interactive Reader and Study Guide

Studying the Ancient World

HISTORY–SOCIAL SCIENCE STANDARDS

HSS 6.1 Students describe what is known through archaeological studies of the early physical and cultural development of humankind from the Paleolithic era to the agricultural revolution.

HSS Analysis Skill HI 5 Students recognize that interpretations of history are subject to change as new information is uncovered.

CHAPTER SUMMARY

Historians
find clues in ↓

court documents
_____
_____
_____

Archaeologists
find clues in ↓

ancient bones
_____
_____
_____

COMPREHENSION AND CRITICAL THINKING

Use the answers to the following questions to fill in the graphic organizer above.

1. Identify Name four items that historians use to find clues.

_____

_____

2. Make Inferences What might an archaeologist learn from ancient bones? What other artifacts would an archeologist study?

_____

_____

3. Develop Write a question that historians could answer based on an old letter.

_____

_____

Studying the Ancient World

MAIN IDEAS

1. Historians and archaeologists look for clues in written records and artifacts.

2. Other sources of clues include legends and luck.

HSS 6.1

Students describe what is known through archeological studies of the early physical and cultural development of humankind from the Paleolithic era to the agricultural revolution.

Key Terms and People

history the study of the past

primary source an account of an event created by someone who took part in or witnessed the event

secondary source information gathered by someone who did not take part in or witness an event

archaeology the study of the past based on materials that people have left behind

fossil a part or imprint of something that was once alive

artifacts objects created and used by humans

Section Summary

WHAT HISTORIANS DO

Historians want to find out how individuals lived. They also consider how groups of people have behaved. **History** is about both the recent and distant past. A **primary source** or a **secondary source** provides clues that answer questions about history. Primary sources include peace treaties, court documents, diaries, and letters. Textbooks and encyclopedias are secondary sources.

The study of history can be difficult, like putting together a puzzle with many pieces missing. Historians want to find out how, when, where, and why individuals and groups behaved as they did.

Name some examples of primary sources.

_____

_____

_____

What can make the study of history difficult?

_____

_____

_____

WHAT ARCHAEOLOGISTS DO

Archaeology also yields information about the past. Archaeologists practice archaeology. They examine **fossil** remains, such as old bones and footprints in rock, to gain information about life in ancient times.

Archaeologists look at **artifacts** made by humans to gather more information. Examples of artifacts are arrowheads, coins, and tools. The term material culture describes collections of related artifacts. The places where artifacts are located yield more information about how people used them.

> **What artifacts might be left behind from our time?**
> _____
> _____
> _____
> _____

OTHER SOURCES OF CLUES

Historians and archaeologists cooperate to learn about history. Written sources help archaeologists find sites where artifacts are located. Material culture helps historians understand what they read.

> **What helps historians understand what they read?**
> _____
> _____

Stories and legends sometimes aid historians and archaeologists in making discoveries. For example, you have probably heard or read stories about King Arthur. No such king lived during the Middle Ages. However, because of the legends surrounding King Arthur, historians have searched old documents for information about England's past. These documents show that a warrior who lived in about the 500s AD might have inspired the legends.

Clues that may lead to amazing finds are inspired by legends. Scholars are still searching in Mongolia for the tomb of conqueror Genghis Khan, basing their work on the legend of his burial.

Even luck plays a part in historical and archaeological finds. At times people digging in fields have unearthed artifacts of historical and archaeological importance.

> **How can luck play a role in history and archaeology?**
> _____
> _____
> _____

CHALLENGE ACTIVITY

Critical Thinking: Elaborating List at least five artifacts that you would leave to help future historians and archaeologists understand your life. Write a brief essay explaining why you would leave each item. **HSS Analysis Skills HI 5**

Studying the Ancient World

MAIN IDEAS

1. Using the evidence they have gathered allows historians to draw conclusions about societies in the past.

2. Views of the past change because of new discoveries and new interpretations.

 HSS 6.1
Students describe what is known through archeological studies of the early physical and cultural development of humankind from the Paleolithic era to the agricultural revolution.

Key Terms and People

society a community of people who share a common culture
social structure the way that people in a group set up their communities

Academic Vocabulary

purpose use or function

Section Summary

USING THE EVIDENCE

Archaeologists, historians, and other experts question what happened in the past. They collect clues and study them to reveal information about past societies. Finding out about a **society** involves studying its **social structure**. Families play a key role in social structure. Literature and art often reveal a lot about family life in past societies.

Politicians' speeches tell us about the politics of the past. The speeches of Greek politicians show that the Greeks valued democracy and freedom. Clues also exist in artifacts. If Roman coins are found in China and Chinese coins in Rome, historians can figure out that the Romans and Chinese had an economic connection.

What can historians learn about past societies by studying their social structures?

_____

_____

_____

BELIEFS AND VALUES

Many sources reveal a society's beliefs and values. The teachings of Confucius show the family's importance in Chinese society. Translating ancient languages is hard for historians. The best-known example of how this can work lies in the Rosetta Stone of Egypt. It contains the same message in Greek and in two kinds of Egyptian writing. Scholars could read Greek and that made translating the message possible.

A society's art may reveal its religious beliefs. Egyptians placed valuable items such as furniture and jewelry in tombs. That evidence teaches that Egyptians believed in life after death. Architecture also suggests certain facts about a society. Greek statues of athletes suggest that the Greeks valued sports. At times archaeologists find items whose **purpose** is not obvious. Experts often disagree on the meaning of these objects.

> **Name three clues used in the study of the past.**
> _____
> _____
> _____

NEW DISCOVERIES

What we think about history is always changing. New historical evidence can give us new information about when events occurred. Very old human bones discovered in Africa and the Americas tell us that human development may have happened much earlier than had been thought.

New archaeological finds can revise our view of history. Scholars once believed that the Maya were peaceful, but recent findings of their writings show that Maya rulers often warred with their neighbors.

> **How can human bones teach us about history?**
> _____
> _____
> _____

NEW INTERPRETATIONS

Historians change their views based on the time, place, and culture within which they live. We now see that women played key roles in U.S. history, but in the past their contributions drew little notice. An open, curious mind is necessary to help historians consider new evidence in evaluating the past.

> **Why do historians sometimes change their views?**
> _____
> _____
> _____

CHALLENGE ACTIVITY

Critical Thinking: Designing Design a time capsule to enclose six objects from your classroom. The capsule will be opened in 1,000 years. Explain why each item should be included. **HSS Analysis Skills HI 5**

Name _____ Class _____ Date _____

The Fall of Rome

HISTORY–SOCIAL SCIENCE STANDARDS
HSS 7.1 Students analyze the causes and effects of the vast expansion and ultimate disintegration of the Roman Empire.
Analysis Skill HSS HI 4 Recognize the role of chance, oversight, and error in history.

CHAPTER SUMMARY

Tables of Similarities and Differences in the Roman Empire

	Western Empire	Eastern Empire
Capital		Constantinople
Religious leaders	popes and bishops	
Political leaders		emperor
Date of fall	476	
Conquered by		Ottoman Turks

COMPREHENSION AND CRITICAL THINKING

Use the answers to the following questions to fill in the graphic organizer above.

1. Explain Why was the Roman Empire divided into the east and the west?

_____

2. Identify Cause and Effect Why did the eastern empire last longer than the western empire?

_____

3. Evaluate Give at least two examples of how the people of the eastern empire were different than those in the western empire.

_____

4. Draw a Conclusion Would you have rather lived in the eastern empire or the western empire? Explain your answer.

_____

_____

Interactive Reader and Study Guide

The Fall of Rome

MAIN IDEAS

1. Leadership and laws helped the Romans build a strong empire.
2. Roman advancements in engineering, architecture, art, and philosophy helped shape later civilizations.
3. Romans helped preserve and spread Christianity.

 HSS 7.1
Students analyze the causes and effects of the vast expansion and ultimate disintegration of the Roman Empire.

Key Terms and People

Augustus first emperor of Rome

citizens people allowed to participate in government

aqueducts channels built to carry water from mountains to cities

Academic Vocabulary

innovation a new idea or way of doing something

Section Summary

BUILDING THE EMPIRE

Between the 700s BC and the 200s AD, Rome grew from a small village to a huge city with over a million inhabitants. Millions more lived in territory controlled by the Romans.

As its territory grew, Rome changed from rule by kings to a government of elected leaders known as a republic. For hundreds of years, the republic grew strong and powerful. Eventually, however, the culture of Rome broke down. To restore order, the Romans changed their government again and became an empire.

An empire is ruled by a powerful leader, who is usually called an emperor. Rome's first emperor, **Augustus**, established the emperor's considerable powers. Some later emperors used this power for good, while others abused it. The Roman empire's

> Underline the phrase that explains why Rome switched governments from an elected republic to an empire ruled by a powerful leader.

laws protected the rights of Roman **citizens**, the people allowed to participate in government. Citizens had both rights and responsibilities. Citizenship of Rome was considered a great honor. Sometimes even people of a newly conquered land would be granted citizenship as a way of ensuring their loyalty to the empire.

> Why do you think Roman citizenship was considered such a great honor?
> _____
> _____
> _____
> _____

ADVANCING CIVILIZATION

The Romans made lasting advances in engineering, architecture, art, and philosophy. Engineers built many roads and made other **innovations** in the infrastructure to make life easier. For example, they built **aqueducts**, channels built to carry water from distant mountain ranges into Rome. They also used their engineering skills to design and construct bigger, better, and more beautiful public buildings. Roman art carried forward the Greek attempts to recreate realistic work.

> Underline one way Roman engineers made life easier for people living in Rome.

Roman philosophy differed from that of the Greeks. Instead of projecting ideal worlds, the Romans focused on more practical ways to improve people's lives. The Stoics, for example, believed that to be happy, one must not focus on possessions, but should act for the good of the group.

> In general, how did Roman philosophers differ from Greek philosophers?
> _____
> _____
> _____

SPREADING CHRISTIANITY

At first, Romans were opposed to the new offshoot of Judaism preached by Jesus. But the religion was popular. Eventually an emperor converted and Christianity became the official religion of the empire. In the later Roman Empire, Christian religious leaders became politically powerful.

> Were Christians persecuted in the later Roman Empire?
> _____
> _____

CHALLENGE ACTIVITY

Critical Thinking: Drawing Inferences In some key ways, the United States has followed the principles of the Roman Empire. Write an essay explaining what similarities you see between ancient Rome and the United States. **HSS Analysis Skills CR 1, CR 3, HI 3**

The Fall of Rome

MAIN IDEAS

1. Many problems threatened the Roman Empire, leading one emperor to divide it in half.

2. Barbarians invaded Rome in the 300s and 400s.

3. Many factors contributed to Rome's fall.

 HSS 7.1
Students analyze the causes and effects of the vast expansion and ultimate disintegration of the Roman Empire.

Key Terms and People

Diocletian emperor who divided the Roman Empire into two parts

Clovis Frankish king who built a huge kingdom in Gaul

Attila fearsome Hun leader who attacked Rome's eastern empire

corruption decay in people's values

Section Summary

PROBLEMS THREATEN THE EMPIRE

At its height, the Roman Empire stretched from Britain south to Egypt, and from the Atlantic Ocean to the Persian Gulf. But by the end of the 100s, emperors had to give up much of that land. The empire was too big to manage well.

Rome had to defend itself constantly. Attacks came from Germany in the north and from Persia in the east. Problems came from within the empire, too. Disease killed many people. Taxes were high. Food was scarce because so many farmers went to war. To increase food production, German farmers were invited to work on Roman lands, but they were not loyal to Rome. Rebellions soon followed.

The emperor **Diocletian** took power in the late 200s. His solution to Rome's problems was to split the empire into two parts. Diocletian ruled the east. He appointed a co-emperor to rule the west. The Emperor Constantine briefly reunited the empire.

> Name three problems facing the Roman Empire around 200.
> _____
> _____
> _____
> _____

> Underline the phrase that explains why the Roman Empire began running out of food.

> Do you think Diocletian's decision to divide the Roman Empire made sense? Why or why not?
> _____
> _____
> _____
> _____

Interactive Reader and Study Guide

Section 2, *continued*

He moved the capital from Rome to a new city he built in the east. He named the city Constantinople, which means "the city of Constantine."

BARBARIANS INVADE ROME

Once the capital moved to the eastern empire, German barbarians started more attacks on Roman territory in the north. During the late 300s, an Asian group called the Huns began attacking a group called the Goths. As the Huns pushed farther into Goth territory, the Goths were forced into Roman territory. Eventually the Goths penetrated deep into Italy and destroyed Rome.

After the destruction of Rome, more groups began invading Roman territory. The Angles, Saxons, and Jutes invaded Britain. The Franks invaded Gaul. The Frankish king **Clovis**, one of the most powerful German kings, built a large kingdom in Gaul. Meanwhile the east was menaced by a fearsome new Hun leader named **Attila**.

In 476 another barbarian leader overthrew the Roman emperor and declared himself king. This ended the western empire.

> Attila the Hun is one of the most notorious figures in history. Why do you think this is so?
>
> _____
> _____
> _____
> _____

FACTORS IN ROME'S FALL

Barbarian invasions were not the only causes of Rome's fall. The empire was too big, making it difficult to rule efficiently. The government also suffered from **corruption**. As these problems grew, wealthy landowners left Rome. They preferred to build armies and protect their personal estates. Only the poor were left in the city. Rome was no longer the great center it had once been.

> A famous phrase says "power corrupts." Do you think this is true? Why or why not?
>
> _____
> _____
> _____
> _____

CHALLENGE ACTIVITY

Critical Thinking: Drawing Inferences Was there anything Roman rulers could have done to stop the disintegration of the western empire or was it's fall inevitable? Write a one-page essay explaining your answer.
HSS Analysis Skills CS 1, HR 5, HI 1

The Fall of Rome

Section 3

> **MAIN IDEAS**
> 1. Eastern emperors ruled from Constantinople and tried but failed to reunite the whole Roman Empire.
> 2. The people of the eastern empire created a new society that was very different from society in the west.
> 3. Byzantine Christianity was different from religion in the west.

 HSS 7.1
Students analyze the causes and effects of the vast expansion and ultimate disintegration of the Roman Empire.

Key Terms and People

Justinian last ruler of the Roman Empire
Theodora Justinian's wife, a wise woman who advised her husband during his reign
Byzantine Empire civilization that developed in the eastern Roman Empire
mosaics pictures made with pieces of colored glass and stone

Section Summary

EMPERORS RULE FROM CONSTANTINOPLE

Constantinople lay between the Black Sea and Mediterranean Sea. This location between the two seas protected Constantinople from attack and helped the city control trade between Europe and Asia. As Rome fell, Constantinople grew.

> Constantinople is now called Istanbul. Find its location in a world atlas. Why do you think it developed as a major trade center?
> _____
> _____
> _____
> _____

Justinian, an eastern emperor who took power in the 500s, wanted to reunite the Roman Empire. His armies managed to recapture Italy. He earned respect for updating, simplifying, and writing down Roman laws, making them more fair. But he made enemies who tried to overthrow him. Justinian got advice from his wife **Theodora**, and was able to stop the riots and keep his throne.

> Who was Justinian's most trusted advisor?
> _____
> _____

Despite Justinian's success, later emperors could not fight off barbarian attacks or hold onto the land. The eastern empire lasted for another 700 years after Justianian's death, but Constantinople was conquered by the Ottoman Turks in 1453.

Section 3, *continued*

A NEW SOCIETY

Justinian is considered the last Roman emperor. After Justinian's death, people in the eastern empire began to follow Greek culture instead of Roman culture. The cultural ties to Rome were slowly lost.

Constantinople was a major trade route among Europeans, Africans, and Asians. Because of this, the people of Constantinople were exposed to new ideas from other cultures. They blended those ideas with their own Roman and Greek roots. Historians call the new society that developed in the east the **Byzantine Empire**. Byzantine culture developed its own distinct features. An eastern emperor, for example, was head of both the church and the government. In the west, popes and bishops ruled the church, but the emperor held political power.

> Why is Justinian considered the "last Roman emperor?"
> _____
> _____
> _____
> _____

BYZANTINE CHRISTIANITY

Christianity was central to the Byzantine Empire. It was illegal to practice any other religion. Artwork dealt with religious themes. Byzantine artists of the period are know for making spectacular **mosaics**, pictures that are made from pieces of colored glass and stone.

For hundreds of years the church leaders of the east and west worked together. Shortly after 1000, the church split in two. Christians in the east formed what is known as the Eastern Orthodox Church. This religious division opened a huge cultural gap between eastern and western Europe.

> Underline the name of the only legally practiced religion in the Byzantine Empire.

> Some historians believe that the well-known historical division between the "eastern" and "western" worlds begins in Byzantine culture. Do you think this so? Why or why not?
> _____
> _____
> _____
> _____

CHALLENGE ACTIVITY

Critical Thinking: Drawing Inferences Imagine that you are Theodora, the wife of Roman Emperor Justinian. You think your husband is making a mistake when he says he wants to leave his kingdom because his enemies have started a riot and threaten to kill him. As a woman you have no power to rule the land. So how would you persuade him to stay and solve the problems with his enemies? Write your answer in the style of a verbal appeal, or speech, you would make to Justinian. **HSS Analysis Skills CR 1, CR 5, HI 4**

Interactive Reader and Study Guide

The Rise of Islam

HISTORY–SOCIAL SCIENCE STANDARDS

HSS 7.2 Students analyze the geographic, political, economic, religious, and social structures of the civilizations of Islam in the Middle Ages.

CHAPTER SUMMARY

Mohammad became a prophet	*because*	1. _____ 2. he taught his beliefs to others.
Some rejected Mohammad's teachings	*because*	1. Arabians had worshipped many gods. 2. _____
The rise of Islam led to social change	*because*	1. charity was expected in Islam. 2. _____

COMPREHENSION AND CRITICAL THINKING

Use the answers to the following questions to fill in the graphic organizer above.

1. Explain From where did Muhammad believe his teachings came?

_____

_____

2. Identify Cause and Effect Who initially rejected what Muhammad had to say? Why?

_____

_____

3. Draw a Conclusion What impact did Muhammad's teachings have upon Arabia's social conditions?

_____

_____

The Rise of Islam

MAIN IDEAS
1. Arabia is mostly a desert land.
2. Two ways of life—nomadic and sedentary—developed in the desert.

HSS 7.2
Students analyze the geographic, political, economic, religious, and social structures of the civilizations of Islam in the Middle Ages.

Key Terms and People

sand dunes hills of sand shaped by the wind

oasis a wet, fertile area in the desert

sedentary settled

caravan a group of traders that travels together

souk a market or bazaar

Academic Vocabulary

features characteristics

Section Summary

A DESERT LAND

The Arabian Peninsula is a mostly hot and dry desert of scorching temperatures and little water. Yet people have lived there for thousands of years.

Arabia, located in the southwest corner of Asia, is the crossroads for three continents—Africa, Europe, and Asia. Trade routes cross the region by both land and sea. These routes have brought many different people and customs through Arabia, influencing the people who live there.

The world's largest sand desert, the Rub' al-Khali (ROOB ahl-KAH-lee), lies in Arabia. This desert is not an easy place to live. **Sand dunes**, or hills of sand shaped by the wind, can rise to 800 feet and stretch for hundreds of miles. Water is scarce and exists mainly in places called an **oasis**, a wet, fertile area in the desert. Oases are key stops along Arabia's trade routes.

Most of Arabia's settlements have been in the mountainous areas that border the southern and

> Arabia was the trading crossroads for what three continents?
>
> _____
> _____
> _____
> _____

> Underline the word that is the plural of "oasis."

Interactive Reader and Study Guide

western coasts, or the flat, marshy land near the
Persian Gulf.

TWO WAYS OF LIFE

People developed two ways to live in the desert.
Nomads moved from place to place. Others chose a
sedentary life in a settlement. Nomads lived in tents
and raised goats, sheep, and camels. They traveled
with their animals along regular routes, depending
upon where they could feed and water the herd.
They traveled in tribes, or groups of people.
Membership in a tribe was important to a nomad.
It provided protection from danger and reduced
competition for grazing lands.

> Why would a nomad prefer to travel in a tribe?
>
> _____
> _____
> _____

Sedentary people lived in the towns and cities
that sprang up in oases along the trade routes.
Merchants and craftspeople traded their goods
through groups of merchants who traveled together
in **caravans**. Most town centers **featured** a **souk**
(SOOK), a market or bazaar, used by both nomads
and caravans.

> Circle the definition of the word souk.

Nearly anything could be found at a souk.
Nomads offered animal products. Caravan
merchants offered clothing, silk, and other goods
from the various kingdoms and civilizations that
used the trade routes. Bargaining was common in
souks, with few set prices. The larger souks would
have roofs. Many stayed open all day.

The souk was a social gathering place as well as
a market. Exposure to the ideas of so many other
cultures deeply influenced Arabian society,
particularly with regard to religion.

CHALLENGE ACTIVITY

Critical Thinking: Drawing Inferences If you lived in Arabia, would you
choose a nomadic or sedentary life? Write a one-page description of
what your life would be like, based on the lifestyle that you would prefer
to live. **HSS Analysis Skills CR 2, HI 1**

The Rise of Islam

MAIN IDEAS

1. Muhammad became a prophet and introduced a religion called Islam in Arabia.
2. Muhammad's teachings had similarities to Judaism and Christianity, but they also presented new ideas.
3. Islam spread in Arabia after being rejected at first.

 HSS 7.2

Students analyze the geographic, political, economic, religious, and social structures of the civilizations of Islam in the Middle Ages.

Key Terms and People

Muhammad an Arabian merchant turned prophet whose teachings became the basis for a new religion

Islam religion based on messages Muhammad received from God

Muslim a person who follows Islam

Qur'an the holy book of Islam

shrine a place where people worship a saint or god

pilgrimage journey to a sacred place

mosque a building for Muslim prayer

Academic Vocabulary

influence change, or have an effect on

Section Summary

MUHAMMAD BECOMES A PROPHET

A man named **Muhammad** brought a new religion to Arabia. Much of what is known about him comes from religious writings.

> Circle the name of Islam's prophet and founder.

Muhammad was born into an important merchant family in the city of Mecca around 570. He was an orphan by the age of six. Male relatives who traveled in caravans raised Muhammad. As an adult, Muhammad managed a caravan business owned by a wealthy woman named Khadijah (ka-DEE-jah). He later married Khadijah.

Muhammad was disturbed to see that the rich people in Mecca did not help the poor. He would often go to a cave and meditate on this problem.

Section 2, *continued*

According to Islamic belief, when Muhammad was 40, an angel began to speak to him. He later began to teach what the angel told him to others. The messages Muhammad received form the basis of a religion called **Islam**. People who practice Islam are called **Muslims**. These messages were collected in the **Qur'an** (kuh-RAN), the holy book of Islam.

> Where did Muhammad first start hearing from an angel of God?
> _____
> _____

MUHAMMAD'S TEACHINGS

Not all of Muhammad's teachings were new. Some of his ideas came from Judaism and Christianity. For example, Muhammad taught that there was only one God—Allah. Muhammad also accepted the teachings of many of the Hebrew prophets.

Monotheism, the belief in only one god, was a new idea that upset many Arabs. Arabs worshipped many gods at **shrines**, places where people honor a saint or god. The most important shrine was in Mecca. Many people traveled to Mecca every year on a **piligrimage**. Muhammad also taught that rich and poor were equal. He said that the rich should give money to the poor. Many rich merchants in Mecca rejected this idea.

> What basic idea of God or the gods do Judaism, Christianity, and Islam all have in common?
> _____
> _____

> Why do you think the rich merchants disliked being told they should give money to the poor?
> _____
> _____

ISLAM SPREADS IN ARABIA

Slowly, Muhammad's message took hold. The rich and powerful were threatened by its influence. Muhammed left Mecca for Medina, a city that promised to protect him. His house became the first **mosque**, or building for Muslim prayer. Here he revealed new rules for Islam. Many desert tribes were converted. Eventually, the tribes began to threaten and attack Mecca's caravans. The people of Mecca gave in and accepted Islam.

> Who made the first rules for practicing Islam?
> _____
> _____

CHALLENGE ACTIVITY

Critical Thinking: Drawing Inferences Pretend that you are Muhammad and you must convince people that they must believe in just one god, and that the rich and poor are equal. Write a persuasive speech that you might give. Speak as if you were talking to people during Muhammad's time. **HSS Analysis Skills CR 2, HI 1, HI 3**

The Rise of Islam

MAIN IDEAS

1. The Qur'an guides Muslims' lives.
2. The Sunnah tells Muslims of important duties expected of them.
3. Islamic law is based on the Qur'an and the Sunnah.

 HSS 7.2
Students analyze the geographic, political, economic, religious, and social structures of the civilizations of Islam in the Middle Ages.

Key Terms and People

jihad literally means "to make an effort, or to struggle"
Sunnah refers to the way Muhammad lived, which provides a model for Muslims
Five Pillars of Islam the five acts of worship required of all Muslims

Section Summary

THE QUR'AN

After Muhammad died, religious leaders wrote down all of the messages he received from Allah. This collection of teachings became known as the Qur'an. Muslims believe that the Qur'an is the exact word of God as it was told to Muhammad. Like the Jewish and Christian bibles, the Qur'an says there is one God (Allah). Islam teaches that there is a definite beginning and end to the world. On that final day, Muslims believe, God will judge all people. Those who have obeyed God's orders will be granted life in paradise. Those who have not obeyed God will be punished.

> Circle the name of Islam's most important holy book.

Muslims believe that God wishes them to follow many rules in order to be judged a good person. These rules affect the everyday life of Muslims. In the early days of Islam, these rules led to great changes in Arabian society. For example, owning slaves was forbidden.

Jihad (ji-HAHD) is an important Islamic concept. Literally, jihad means "to make an effort, or to struggle." It refers to the internal struggle of a Muslim trying to follow Islamic beliefs. It can also

> How do you think "jihad" came to mean "holy war?"
> _____
> _____
> _____
> _____

Name _____ Class _____ Date _____

Section 3, *continued*

mean the struggle to defend the Muslim community
or convert people to Islam. The word has also been
translated as "holy war."

THE SUNNAH

Another important component of Islamic faith
is the **Sunnah** (SOOH-nuh), or the example of
right behavior provided by Muhammad's life and
teachings. From the Sunnah are derived the main
duties for Muslims, known as the **Five Pillars of
Islam**. The first pillar is a statement of faith. The
second pillar says a Muslim must pray five times
daily. The third pillar is a yearly donation to charity.
The fourth pillar is fasting during the holy month
of Ramadan (RAH-muh-dahn). The fifth pillar is the
hajj (HAJ), a pilgrimage to Mecca that must be made
at least once in a lifetime.

The Sunnah also preaches moral duties that must
be met in daily life. It is considered immoral and
wrong to owe someone money, for example, or to
disobey a leader.

> **Do Muslims believe that the Sunnah is the direct word of God?**
> _____
> _____

> **What is the third pillar of Islam?**
> _____
> _____
> _____

ISLAMIC LAW

The Qur'an and the Sunnah form the basis of
Islamic law, or Shariah (shuh-REE-uh). Shariah lists
rewards or punishments for obeying or disobeying
laws. Shariah punishments can be severe. Shariah
makes no distinction between religious and secular
life. Most Islamic countries also use a court system
much like that in the United States to deal with
non-religious matters. In some traditional Islamic
countries, however, Shariah is very influential in
daily life.

> **Is Shariah the only law used in Islamic countries?**
> _____
> _____

CHALLENGE ACTIVITY

Critical Thinking: Drawing Inferences Write a brief essay evaluating the
differences and similarities between the two earlier religions of Judaism
and Christianity with Islam. Focus not only on beliefs but also on
practices and what social conditions might have influenced these
practices in all the religions. **HSS Analysis Skills CR 5, HI 2**

Interactive Reader and Study Guide

The Spread of Islam

HISTORY–SOCIAL SCIENCE STANDARDS
HSS 7.2 Students analyze the geographic, political, economic, religious, and social structures of the civilizations of Islam in the Middle Ages.
HSS Analysis Skill HR 1 Frame questions for study and research.
HR 5 Determine the context in which statements were made.

CHAPTER SUMMARY

Effects of Spread of Islam	
	Examples of Islamic Impact
Arabia	Unified for first time
Social Change	
Byzantine Empire	Overcame by Ottoman Turks
Science, Medicine, and Mathematics	
Arts	*The Thouand and One Nights*, Taj Mahal

COMPREHENSION AND CRITICAL THINKING

Use the answers to the following questions to fill in the graphic organizer above.

1. Explain Who was the first caliph? What did he accomplish?

_____

2. Identify Cause and Effect What was the impact of Islam on early Arabian society?

_____

_____

3. Evaluate Name three great achievements of Islamic empires.

_____

_____

4. Draw a Conclusion Were the Islamic empires a good place to live if you were a woman or a non-Muslim? Explain.

_____

_____

The Spread of Islam

Section 1

MAIN IDEAS

1. Muslim armies conquered many lands into which Islam slowly spread.
2. Trade helped Islam spread into new areas.
3. A mix of cultures was one result of Islam's spread.
4. Islamic influence encouraged the growth of cities.

 HSS 7.2
Students analyze the geographic, political, economic, religious, and social structures of the civilizations of Islam in the Middle Ages.

Key Terms and People

Abu Bakr one of Islam's first converts, appointed caliph after Muhammad's death

caliph title of the highest Islamic leader

tolerance acceptance

Section Summary

MUSLIM ARMIES CONQUER MANY LANDS

After Muhammad's death his followers quickly chose **Abu Bakr** (uh-boo BAK-uhr), one of Muhammad's first converts, to be the next leader of Islam. He was the first **caliph** (KAY-luhf), a title reserved for the highest Islamic leader.

As caliph, Abu Bakr was a political and military leader, but not a religious leader. Through many battles, he unified Arabia for the first time. The new united Arab army quickly conquered the Persian and Byzantine empires. The Muslims made a pact with the non-Muslims they controlled. Other religions were allowed to exist, but only under the pact rules.

The next several caliphs came from the Umayyad (oohm-EYE-yuhd) family. They conquered many tribes in Central Asia and took over kingdoms in northern India. Soon they controlled eastern Mediterranean trade routes and conquered some Byzantine lands in North Africa. The Berbers slowed Muslim expansion into North Africa.

> What is probably the main reason Abu Bakr was named the first Islamic leader after Muhammad's death?
>
> _____
> _____
> _____

> What present-day countries mark the eastern and western boundaries of the Islamic empire?
>
> _____
> _____
> _____

Name _____ Class _____ Date _____

Section 1, *continued*

The Berbers eventually converted to Islam. A combined Arab and Berber army conquered Spain and pushed into France, finally stopping after nearly losing a battle near Tours. Muslims continued to rule parts of Spain for another 700 years.

TRADE HELPS ISLAM SPREAD
Arab merchants took Islamic beliefs and practices with them to new lands. The merchants would bring back new products and inventions. In India and other countries, coastal trading cities developed into large Muslim communities.

> Why do think trade flourishes in coastal cities?
> _____
> _____
> _____
> _____

A MIX OF CULTURES
Muslims generally practiced **tolerance**, or acceptance, of the non-Muslims they encountered through either war or trade. Jews and Christians, who shared some Muslim beliefs, were allowed to practice their own religion, but had to pay a tax.

More people began speaking Arabic, particularly in trading towns. The Arabs took on customs from the countries they conquered. Cultural blending changed Islam from a mostly Arab religion into a religion of many different cultures.

> Underline the phrase that explains why Muslims allowed Jews and Christians to practice their own religions.

THE GROWTH OF CITIES
The growing Muslim cities reflected this blending of cultures. The wealthy city of Baghdad, for example, attracted many artists and writers. Córdoba in Spain was the largest, most advanced European city during the early 900s.

Córdoba also had a thriving Jewish community. Jewish poets, philosophers, and scientists made great contributions to Córdoba's cultural growth.

> What other religious group besides Islam enjoyed a thriving culture in Islamic Spain?
> _____
> _____

CHALLENGE ACTIVITY
Critical Thinking: Drawing Inferences Draw a timeline marking the major Muslim conquests during the Middle Ages. Now draw a map to show the size of Islamic territory and influence at that time. **HSS Analysis Skills CS2, HI 2**

Interactive Reader and Study Guide

The Spread of Islam

MAIN IDEAS

1. The Ottoman Empire covered a large area in eastern Europe.
2. The Safavid Empire blended Persian cultural traditions with Shia Islam.
3. The Mughal Empire in India left an impressive cultural heritage.

 HSS 7.2
Students analyze the geographic, political, economic, religious, and social structures of the civilizations of Islam in the Middle Ages.

Key Terms and People

Janissaries enslaved youths converted to Islam and trained as soldiers
Mehmed II Ottoman ruler who defeated the Byzantine Empire
sultan an Ottoman ruler
Suleyman I Ottoman ruler who led the empire to its heights
harem a separate area of a household where women lived away from men
Shia Muslims who believed only members of Muhammad's family could be caliphs
Sunni Muslims who believed caliphs did not have to be related to Muhammad

Section Summary

THE OTTOMAN EMPIRE

Built on conquest, the Ottoman Empire was a powerful political and cultural force for centuries. It grew from a small kingdom into a large empire.

In the mid-1200s, Muslim Turkish warriors began to take land from the Christian Byzantine Empire. The Ottomans eventually controlled eastern Europe, North Africa, and northern Arabia. **Janissaries**, male youths taken from conquered towns and converted to Islam, fought fiercely in these conquests. The Byzantine Empire came to an end in 1453 when Ottomans led by **Mehmed II** captured Constantinople. A later **sultan** continued Mehmed's conquests. The Ottoman Empire reached its height under **Suleyman I** (soo-lay-MAHN), "the Magnificent." By 1566 the Ottomans took control of the eastern Mediterranean and parts of Europe.

> Underline the phrase that tells where the Ottomans found fierce soldiers to fight in their armies.

> What date signifies the absolute final end of the Roman Empire?
>
> _____
> _____

Ottoman society was divided into two classes. Judges and others who advised the sultan on legal and military matters were part of the ruling class. The ruling class had to be loyal to the sultan, practice Islam, and understand Ottoman customs. The lower classes included many Christians and Jews from lands the Ottomans had conquered.

Ottoman society limited the freedom of women, particularly in the ruling classes. Women had to live apart from men in an area called a **harem**.

THE SAFAVID EMPIRE

Meanwhile, a group of Persian Muslims known as the Safavids (sah-FAH-vuhds) gained power in the east. Before long, the Safavids came into conflict with the Ottomans and other Muslims. The conflict stemmed from an old disagreement about who should be caliph. In the mid-600s, Islam had split into two groups—the **Sunni** and the **Shia**. The Ottomans were Sunni and the Safavids were Shia.

> Think of what you know about the Middle East today. Does the conflict between the Sunnis and the Shias continue?
> _____
> _____

The Safavid Empire conquered Persia in 1501. Under the rule of 'Abbas, the Safavid Empire reached its height.

THE MUGHAL EMPIRE

East of the Safavid Empire, in India, lay the Mughal (MOO-guhl) Empire. Like the Ottomans, the Mughals united many diverse peoples. They left a cultural heritage known for poetry and architecture. Mughal emperor Shah Jahan built the famous Taj Mahal. Under the leader Akbar, the Mughal Empire was known for its religious tolerance. But more restrictive policies after his death led to revolt and ultimately the end of the empire.

> What is the most famous architectural achievement of the Mughal Empire?
> _____
> _____

CHALLENGE ACTIVITY

Critical Thinking: Drawing Inferences Pretend that you are a Janissary, taken into the Ottoman army. Write several journal entries about what might have happened to you and how you feel about it. **HSS Analysis Skills CR 2, HI 1**

The Spread of Islam

Section 3

MAIN IDEAS

1. Muslim scholars made advances in various fields of science and philosophy.
2. Islam influenced styles of literature and the arts.

 HSS 7.2
Students analyze the geographic, political, economic, religious, and social structures of the civilizations of Islam in the Middle Ages.

Key Terms and People

Ibn Battutah Muslim explorer and geographer

Sufism a movement of Islam, based on the belief that one must have a personal relationship with God

Omar Khayyám famous Sufi poet, wrote *The Rubáiyát*

patrons sponsors

minaret a narrow tower on a mosque from which Muslims are called to pray

calligraphy decorative writing

Section Summary

SCIENCE AND PHILOSOPHY

Islamic scholars made great advances in astronomy, geography, math, and science. Scholars at Baghdad and Córdoba translated ancient Greek and other writings on these subjects into Arabic. A common language helped scholars share research.

Scientists built many observatories to further their knowledge of astronomy. Muslim scientists also improved the astrolabe, which the Greeks had invented to chart the position of the stars. The astrolabe would later be used in sea exploration.

As people learned to use the stars to calculate time and location, Muslim merchants and explorers traveled more widely than ever, particularly the great explorer **Ibn Battutah**. Muslim geographers made more accurate maps, and created better ways of calculating distances. It was a Muslim mathematician who invented algebra.

The greatest Islamic advances were in medicine. Muslims added greatly to Greek and Indian

> **Which two cities came to be recognized as the cultural capitals of Islam during the Middle Ages?**
>
> _____
> _____
> _____

> **Why do you think the astrolabe would be useful in sea exploration?**
>
> _____
> _____
> _____
> _____

medicine. They developed tests to qualify doctors before they could treat people. They made the first organized list of drugs and their effects, and started the first school of pharmacy.

A doctor named Ar-Razi discovered how to diagnose and treat the deadly disease smallpox. Another doctor, Ibn-Sina, who was known in the West as Avicenna (av-uh-SEN-uh), wrote a medical encyclopedia that was used widely throughout Europe for centuries.

A new philosophy also developed called **Sufism** (SOO-fi-zuhm). Sufis sought a personal relationship with God.

> Write the names of two famous Muslim doctors who made advances in medicine:
> _____
> _____
> _____

LITERATURE AND THE ARTS

Poetry and short stories were popular among Muslims. The collection of stories called *The Thouand and One Nights* is still one of the best-loved books in the world. Sufi poets were popular, including the famous **Omar Khayyám** (oh-mahr ky-AHM).

> What is the name of Islam's great collection of stories?
> _____
> _____

Architectural achievements included many mosques. Rulers liked to be **patrons** and help to fund the design and construction of beautiful mosques. The main part of a mosque is a huge hall where thousands of people gather to pray. Often mosques have a large dome and a **minaret**.

Islam does not allow artists to show animals or humans. Muslims believe only Allah can create humans and animals or their images. Partly for this reason, Muslim artists turned **calligraphy**, or decorative writing, into an art form.

> Underline the sentence that helps to explain why Muslim artists developed calligraphy as a fine art

CHALLENGE ACTIVITY

Critical Thinking: Drawing Inferences Islamic culture has created many advances in science, medicine, and art that we still use today. Pick the advance that you think is the most important to our modern society, and write a one-page paper explaining your position. **HSS Analysis Skills CS 1, HI 3**

Interactive Reader and Study Guide

Name _____ Class _____ Date _____

Early West African Societies

CHAPTER SUMMARY

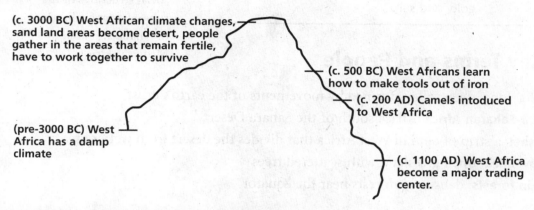

(c. 3000 BC) West African climate changes, sand land areas become desert, people gather in the areas that remain fertile, have to work together to survive

(c. 500 BC) West Africans learn how to make tools out of iron

(c. 200 AD) Camels intoduced to West Africa

(pre-3000 BC) West Africa has a damp climate

(c. 1100 AD) West Africa become a major trading center.

COMPREHENSION AND CRITICAL THINKING

Use information from the graphic organizer to answer the following questions.

1. Explain When and why did Africans first begin to settle in villages?

_____

_____

2. Identify Cause and Effect Why was the extended family important to West African village life?

_____

_____

3. Evaluate What technology changed West African society dramatically. Why?

_____

_____

4. Draw a Conclusion What were the advantages of trading local resources for West African society?

_____

_____

Interactive Reader and Study Guide

Early West African Societies

MAIN IDEAS

1. The landforms, water, climate, and plant life affected history in West Africa.

2. West Africa's resources included farmland, gold, and salt.

 HSS 7.4
Students analyze the geographic, political, economic, religious, and social structures of the sub-Saharan civilizations of Ghana and Mali in Medieval Africa.

Key Terms and People

rifts long, deep valleys formed by movements of the earth's crust

sub-Saharan Africa Africa south of the Sahara Desert

Sahel a strip of land in West Africa that divides the desert from wetter areas

savannah open grassland with scattered trees

rain forests dense, wet forests near the equator

Section Summary

LANDFORMS, WATER, CLIMATE, AND PLANT LIFE

Africa is the second-largest continent in the world, second only to Asia. The vast land is shaped like a soup bowl, ringed with mighty mountain chains. In eastern Africa, mountains extend along **rifts**, long deep valleys that were formed by movements of the earth's crust.

There are large rivers that cross the plains of **sub-Saharan Africa,** the name for Africa south of the Sahara. Great civilizations grew up along the Niger River, one of the rivers flowing through these plains. The Niger River starts close to the Atlantic Ocean and flows for about 2,600 miles before ending in the Gulf of Guinea. The Niger River's middle section is called the inland delta. This part of the river has several low-lying lakes and marshes. Many animals and plants flourish in this area.

Four different regions make up the area around the Niger. The regions, running from east to west, range from very dry and sandy to very wet and green. The northern band is the southern part of

> **What caused the great rift valleys of eastern Africa?**
> _____
> _____
> _____

> **What is the name of the part of the ocean where the Niger River empties?**
> _____
> _____

Interactive Reader and Study Guide

Name _____ Class _____ Date _____

Section 1, *continued*

the Sahara desert, so it is hot and dry here. Next is the **Sahel**, a strip of land that divides the desert from the wetter areas. Then there is the **savannah**, which has open grasslands. Both the Sahel and the savannah can support herds of animals for grazing. The fourth region is **rain forest**, dense, wet area with lots of trees and plants. The rain forests lie near the equator.

> What two areas along the Niger are good for grazing cattle?
>
> _____
> _____
> _____

WEST AFRICA'S RESOURCES

West Africa's farmland is a major resource. Its different climates help grow many different types of crops. These crops include dates from the desert and medicinal kola nuts from the forest. Minerals are also an important resource.

The Sahara Desert has left many salt deposits. Salt was important for people who lived on mainly plant foods, like many early Africans who needed to add salt to their diets. Salt was also a necessary ingredient for curing and preserving meat.

> Underline the two sentences that explain why salt was so valuable to the West Africans.

For centuries, gold came from secret riverbed mines in the forest region. Even today, no one is sure which riverbeds yielded the valuable gold nuggets. But gold was very important for trading.

CHALLENGE ACTIVITY

Critical Thinking: Drawing Inferences Draw a picture of the Niger River, representing the four regions. Draw some animals and plants that might be found in those regions. Now pretend that you are an explorer traveling along the Niger River. Write about your discoveries in a travel logbook. Write at least one entry for each of the Niger River's four regions. **HSS Analysis Skills HR 3, HR 5, HI 4**

Interactive Reader and Study Guide

Early West African Societies

MAIN IDEAS

1. Family and religion influenced daily life in early West African society.
2. Iron technology changed life in West Africa.
3. Trade shaped the history of West Africa.

 HSS 7.4
Students analyze the geographic, political, economic, religious, and social structures of the sub-Saharan civilizations of Ghana and Mali in Medieval Africa.

Key Terms and People

extended family parents, children, and near relatives who all live in one household
animism the belief that bodies of water, animals, trees, and other natural objects have spirits

Academic Vocabulary

traditional customary, time-honored

Section Summary

FAMILIES, RELIGION, AND DAILY LIFE

Thousands of years ago, much of Africa had a wet climate. But the climate in many areas became drier, creating desert. People who used to roam freely had to leave the desert areas. They moved closer together, settling in villages. At the heart of village life was family.

A typical West African family was an **extended family**. In an extended family, parents, children, and near relatives all live in one household. In some areas, men or women born within two to three years of each other formed age-sets. People in extended families and age-sets had a duty to help each other.

Traditional West African beliefs reinforce the importance of the family. Loyalty helped support village life. Everyone worked hard. The men hunted and farmed. They grew versatile grains such as millet and sorghum. The women took care of the children, farmed, gathered firewood, carried water, and ground grain.

> Underline the sentence that explains why West African village life first formed.

> Can you name another group that values the extended family?
> _____
> _____

Interactive Reader and Study Guide

Section 2, *continued*

Religion was also central to West African life. Most villagers believed that the spirits of people who died stayed close to their village. The living would erect statues in honor of their dead ancestors. They would also deliver news to the dead ancestors and offer food to the spirits. Another common belief was **animism**, the belief that animals, trees, bodies of water, and other natural objects have spirits.

> Explain very briefly how the family is central even to West African religion.
> _____
> _____
> _____
> _____
> _____

TECHNOLOGY AND CHANGE

Over time new discoveries changed West African culture. The most imporant discovery happened around 500 BC when West Africans learned how to make tools out of iron. The first people to use this technology were the Nok people. The Nok lived in modern-day Nigeria. They used iron to make better farm tools to grow more food. With iron tools, people could cut down trees and make more land useable for farming. They also used iron to make stronger weapons. With more resources, the people had surpluses that they could trade.

> Circle two ways the Nok people used iron to help their people grow stronger.

TRADE AND WEST AFRICA

At first people had trouble traveling through the African deserts to trade. Around 200 AD, Romans brought the first camels to Africa. Camels could travel a long way in the desert without needing water. People traded gold, salt, cloth, and human slaves. Trade routes went all the way to Europe and to the Islamic world. Some trading camps, like Timbuktu, grew into cities. Timbuktu later become the center of an empire that grew from the riches made from the trade routes across the Sahara.

> What continent do you think the camels first came from?
> _____
> _____

CHALLENGE ACTIVITY

Critical Thinking: Drawing Inferences Early West African culture might seem very different from our modern world. Are there any similarities between the ways the early West Africans lived and the way you live? Write a one-page essay explaining your answer. **HSS Analysis Skills CS 1, HI 1**

West African Empires

HISTORY–SOCIAL SCIENCE STANDARDS
HSS 7.4 Students analyze the geographic, political, economic, religious, and social structures of the sub-Saharan civilizations of Ghana and Mali in Medieval Africa.
HSS Analysis Skill HR 2 Students distinguish fact from opinion in historical narratives and stories.
HSS Analysis Skill CS 3 Use a variety of maps to explain the expansion and disintegration of empires.

CHAPTER SUMMARY

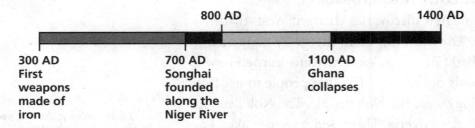

800 AD

1400 AD

300 AD
First
weapons
made of
iron

700 AD
Songhai
founded
along the
Niger River

1100 AD
Ghana
collapses

COMPREHENSION AND CRITICAL THINKING

Use the answers to the following questions to fill in the graphic organizer above.

1. **Explain** Why did the first Africans live together in extended families, or age-set groups?

_____

_____

2. **Identify Cause and Effect** How did Ghana become the first West African empire?

_____

_____

3. **Evaluate** What was Mansa Musa's impact on West African culture?

_____

_____

4. **Draw a Conclusion** What was the biggest change in West African culture with the onset of the various empires?

_____

_____

West African Empires

Section 1

MAIN IDEAS

1. Ghana controlled trade and became wealthy.
2. Through its control of trade, Ghana built an empire.
3. Ghana's decline was caused by attacking invaders, overgrazing, and the loss of trade.

 HSS 7.4

Students analyze the geographic, political, economic, religious, and social structures of the sub-Saharan civilizations of Ghana and Mali in Medieval Africa.

Key Terms and People

silent barter a process in which people exchange goods without ever contacting each other directly

Tunka Manin Ghana's king who ruled the empire at the height of its power

Academic Vocabulary

process a series of steps by which a task is accomplished

Section Summary

GHANA CONTROLS TRADE

Ghana (GAH-nuh) was the first West African empire to profit from Saharan trade by controlling trade routes. Ghana lay between the Niger and Senegal rivers in sub-Saharan Africa, northwest of the nation now called Ghana.

Historians think the first people in Ghana were farmers. Starting around 300 these farmers began to be threatened by nomadic herders who wanted the water and pastures. For protection, small groups began to band together. This cooperation grew stronger with the introduction of farming tools and weapons made of iron.

Ghana's territory lay between the desert and the forests, areas rich with salt and gold. The gold and salt trade followed a **process** called **silent barter**, in which people exchange goods without contacting each other directly. This ensured peaceful business and kept the location of the gold mines secret.

> What economic factor was Ghana the first in West Africa to exploit?
> _____
> _____

> Which was more valuable, salt or gold? Why?
> _____
> _____

Section 1, *continued*

The rulers of Ghana, strengthened by trade and increased populations, took control of the trade routes previously run by local tribes. A large trading city, Koumbi Saleh (KOOM-bee SAHL-uh), became a regular travelers' stop.

> Write the name of Ghana's great trading city.
>
> _____
>
> _____

GHANA BUILDS AN EMPIRE

By 800 Ghana was firmly in control of West Africa's trade routes. As a result, trade became safer and Ghana's influence increased. Traders were charged a tax to enter or leave Ghana. The kings made it illegal for anyone other than themselves to own gold. They also taxed the people of Ghana.

> When the kings made it illegal for anyone else to own gold, what happened to the value of gold? Explain.
>
> _____
>
> _____

The kings increased the size of Ghana by conquering other tribes. However, Ghana's kings allowed local conquered rulers to retain much of their own power. These kings acted as governors of their territories. The empire of Ghana reached its peak under **Tunka Manin** (TOOHN-kah MAH-nin).

GHANA'S DECLINE

By the end of the 1000s, Ghana had collapsed. Three major factors contributed to its decline. A group of Muslim Berbers called the Almoravids invaded and weakened the empire. These Berbers were herders, and their animals overgrazed and ruined the farmland. Many farmers left. At the same time, internal rebellions led to Ghana's loss of control over trade routes.

> List two reasons for the decline of Ghana's empire.
>
> _____
>
> _____
>
> _____

CHALLENGE ACTIVITY

Critical Thinking: Drawing Inferences Recreate the silent barter system in the classroom. Divide students into groups of gold and salt traders. Each group of "traders" should write a one-page paper detailing the advantages and disadvantages of silent barter. **HSS Analysis Skills CS 3, HI 6**

West African Empires

Section 2

> **MAIN IDEAS**
> 1. A ruler named Sundiata made Mali into an empire.
> 2. Mali reached its height under the ruler Mansa Musa.
> 3. Mali fell to invaders in the late 1400s.

 HSS 7.4
Students analyze the geographic, political, economic, religious, and social structures of the sub-Saharan civilizations of Ghana and Mali in Medieval Africa.

Key Terms and People

Sundiata ruler that led the Mali Empire's rise to power

Mansa Musa Muslim king who ruled the Mali Empire at the height of its power and spread Islam through a large part of Africa

Section Summary

SUNDIATA MAKES MALI AN EMPIRE

Like Ghana, Mali (MAH-lee) lay along the upper Niger River. This area's fertile soil helped Mali grow. In addition, Mali's location on the Niger River allowed its people to control trade on the river. Mali's rise to power began under a ruler named **Sundiata** (soohn-JAHT-ah).

> What river flowed through both Ghana and Mali?

Many legends about this period claim that Sundiata was both a warrior and a magician. According to these legends, Sundiata was a son of the king of Mali. A cruel ruler conquered Mali when Sundiata was a boy. When Sundiata grew older, he gathered a huge army and won Mali's independence. Then he conquered nearby kingdoms, including Ghana, and took over the salt and gold trades.

Sundiata rebuilt the overgrazed farmlands. He introduced new crops like cotton. He put soldiers to work in the fields. He also took over both the religious and political authority previously held by local leaders.

> Name two of the measures Sundiata took in order to restore the farmlands.
>
> _____
> _____
> _____
> _____

MANSA MUSA

Mali's greatest and most famous ruler was a Muslim named **Mansa Musa** (MAHN-sah moo-SAH). Under his leadership, Mali reached the height of its wealth, power, and fame. Because of Mansa Musa's influence, Islam spread through a large part of West Africa.

> **Why do you think Mansa Musa is regarded as Africa's first great diplomat?**
> _____
> _____
> _____
> _____
> _____

Mansa Musa ruled Mali for about 25 years, during which he captured many important trading cities. He also made the world aware of Mali by making his pilgrimage to Mecca, where he introduced himself to every official he met.

Mansa Musa sent scholars to study the Qur'an and Arabic in Morocco. He established Arabic schools in Mali, where the Qur'an and other literature were available to all who wanted to study. The Mali capital of Timbuktu (time-buhk-TOO) became a great center of Islamic culture. Arabic became the main language of both religion and government. Mansa Musa built mosques in Mali's cities, but he did not force Islam on anyone who chose not to practice it.

> **Do you think Mali under Mansa Musa was a free society? Why or why not?**
> _____
> _____
> _____
> _____

THE FALL OF MALI

Unfortunately, not all of Mali's leaders were as strong as Munsa Musa. After he died, invaders and uprisings tore apart the large and unwieldy empire. Invaders destroyed the great schools and mosques of Timbuktu. Rebel groups seized the city. By 1500 nearly all of the lands the empire had once ruled were lost.

> **Circle the date by which Mali had lost most of its land and power.**

CHALLENGE ACTIVITY

Critical Thinking: Drawing Inferences You are an Egyptian newspaper reporter who does not know much about Africa. One day the king of the faraway empire of Mali comes through your city on his way to Mecca. You can see his massive caravan. Your talks with local leaders reveal that he has visited them, leaving gifts of gold and making a magnificent impression. Write a newspaper article about this person.
HSS Analysis Skills CR 2, CR 3, CR 4

Interactive Reader and Study Guide

West African Empires

Section 3

```
MAIN IDEAS
  1. The Songhai built a new empire in West
     Africa.
  2. Askia the Great ruled Songhai as an
     Islamic empire.
  3. Songhai fell to Moroccan invaders, ending
     the great era of West African empires
```

 HSS 7.4
Students analyze the
geographic, political,
economic, religious, and
social structures of the
sub-Saharan civilizations
of Ghana and Mali in
Medieval Africa.

Key Terms and People

Sunni Ali first leader of Songhai, the last of the great West African empires

Askia the Great Muslim ruler who led Songhai to the height of its power

Academic Vocabulary

various of many types

Section Summary

THE SONGHAI BUILD AN EMPIRE

As Mali weakened, a people called the Songhai
(SAHNG-hy) grew in strength. These people gave
their name to the last of the great West African
trade empires.

Songhai's founders were Berbers from North
Africa who began settling along the big bend of the
Niger River in the 700s. In this inland delta area,
the river brings precious water to an otherwise dry
region. Soon the settlers had built villages and were
trading on the river. Trade brought the Songhai into
contact with Muslims. By the 1000s, many of the
Songhai had converted to Islam.

In the 1300s the lands of the Songhai lay within
the empire of Mali, which was at the height of its
power. However, the Songhai did not like living
under Mali's rule. As Mali weakened, the Songhai
broke free. Then in 1468, Songhai leader **Sunni Ali**
(SOOH-nee ah-LEE) captured the trade centers of

> **Where did the Songhai originally come from?**
> _____
> _____

> **Who was the Songhai Empire's first leader?**
> _____
> _____

Section 3, *continued*

Timbuktu and Djenné, and eventually all of Mali. He went on to develop trade centers and build up his capital, Gao. From Gao, Sunni Ali made Songhai into an empire famous for its wealth.

ASKIA THE GREAT

Sunni Ali and Sunni Baru, his son who followed him as ruler, were not Muslims. But most of the people of the empire's towns were Muslim. They feared that if Sunni Baru did not support Islam they would lose trade and power, so they rebelled. After overthrowing Sunni Baru, the leader of that rebellion became known as **Askia the Great**.

Muslim culture and education thrived during Askia's reign, as they had under Mansa Musa. Timbuktu's schools of learning were strengthened and began to attract students from as far away as Europe. Djenné also became a center of learning, especially for medical science. Doctors in Djenné discovered that mosquitoes spread malaria.

To rule Songhai effectively, Askia divided the empire into five regions. He created **various** departments in charge of special tasks, much like governments today. He also improved banking methods and standardized currency.

> Who was Sunni Baru's father?
> _____

> What did Mansa Musa and Askia the Great have in common?
> _____

SONGHAI FALLS TO MOROCCO

Askia the Great lost power to his son in 1528. Morocco, a country to the north, invaded Songhai. They attacked and looted both Timbuktu and Gao. Songhai never recovered. Overland trade declined. Other trade centers north and south of the old empire grew and became more important. That completed Songhai's downfall.

> Do research on the Internet or in a library and find the population of Timbuktu today. Write that figure here:
> _____

CHALLENGE ACTIVITY

Critical Thinking: Drawing Inferences Why was it important for the Songhai people that their leaders be Muslim? Write an argument explaining why or why not overthrowing the non-Muslim leader Sunni Baru was justified. **HSS Analysis Skills HR 5, HI 2**

West African Empires

MAIN IDEAS

1. Storytellers helped maintain the oral history of the cultures of West Africa.
2. Visitors to West Africa from other lands wrote histories and descriptions of what they saw there.
3. Traditionally, West Africans have valued the arts.

 HSS 7.4

Students analyze the geographic, political, economic, religious, and social structures of the sub-Saharan civilizations of Ghana and Mali in Medieval Africa.

Key Terms and People

oral history a spoken record of past events

griots West African storytellers responsible for reciting oral history

proverbs short sayings of wisdom or truth

kente handwoven, brightly colored cloth made in West Africa

Section Summary

STORYTELLERS MAINTAIN ORAL TRADITIONS

Although cities like Timbuktu and Djenné were known for their universities and libraries, writing was not common in West Africa. Arabic was the only written language, and those who could read and write it were mainly government and religious officials. Instead of writing their history, West Africans passed along information about their civilization through **oral history** in their native languages.

> **Did Arabic replace the native languages of the West Africans? How do you know your answer is correct?**
> _____
> _____
> _____
> _____

The task of remembering and telling West Africa's history was entrusted to storytellers called **griots** (GREE-ohz). Griots tried to make their stories entertaining. They also told **proverbs**, or short sayings of wisdom or truth. The griots had to memorize hundreds of names and dates. Some griots confused names and events in their heads, so some stories might became distorted. Still, much knowledge could be gained by listening to a griot.

> **Underline the sentence that explains why the history of the griots might not be perfectly accurate.**

Interactive Reader and Study Guide

The histories of empires were often told as epic poems, long poems about kingdoms and heroes.

VISITORS WRITE HISTORIES

Though the West Africans left no written histories, visitors from other parts of the world did write about the region. Much of what we know about early West Africa comes from the writings of travelers and scholars from Muslim lands such as Spain and Arabia. Some of these writers include al-Masudi, al-Bakri, Ibn Battutah, and Leo Africanus.

> Of the four writers listed, which one has a non-Arabic name?
> _____
> _____

WEST AFRICANS VALUE ARTS

Besides storytelling, West African cultures considered other art forms, including sculpture, mask-making, cloth-making, music, and dance just as important. West African artists made sculptures of people from wood, brass, clay, ivory, stone, and other materials. Some of these images have inspired modern artists like Matisse and Picasso.

> Circle the names of the modern artists inspired by the images crafted by West African sculptors.

West Africans are also known for distinctive mask-making and textiles. Particularly prized is the brightly colored **kente** (ken-TAY), a hand-woven cloth that was worn by kings and queens on special occasions.

In many West African societies, music and dance were as important as the visual arts. Singing and dancing were great entertainment, but they also helped people celebrate their history and were central to many religious celebrations.

> List three ways in which music had a place in West African culture.
> _____
> _____
> _____
> _____

CHALLENGE ACTIVITY

Critical Thinking: Drawing Inferences Much of what we know about West Africa comes from oral traditions or accounts by visitors to the land. Write one page evaluating the accuracy of these resources. Which sources are primary, which are secondary? Consider how much a visitor who was not raised in a culture can really understand about that culture. **HSS Analysis Skills CR 2, CR 3, CR 4**

China

HISTORY–SOCIAL SCIENCE STANDARDS
HSS 7.3 Students analyze the geographic, political, economic, religious, and social structures of the civilizations of China of the Middle Ages.

CHAPTER SUMMARY

COMPREHENSION AND CRITICAL THINKING

Use information from the graphic organizer to answer the following questions.

1. Identify From which direction did invaders of China almost always come?

_____

_____

2. Draw inference Confucianism emphasized order in society. Which category of achievement do you think was most influenced by Confucianism?

_____

_____

3. Evaluate Why do you think agricultural achievements such as irrigation and faster-growing crops lead to increased trade?

_____

_____

_____

4. Recall What major world religion exerted a powerful influence on Chinese culture?

_____

_____

China

MAIN IDEAS

1. The Period of Disunion was a time of war and disorder that followed the end of the Han dynasty.

2. China was reunified under the Sui, Tang, and Song dynasties.

3. The Age of Buddhism saw major religious changes in China.

 HSS 7.3
Students analyze the geographic, political, economic, religious, and social structures of the civilizations of China of the Middle Ages.

Key Terms and People

Empress Wu Tang ruler whose methods were sometimes vicious, but whose reign was stable and prosperous

Section Summary

THE PERIOD OF DISUNION

After the Han dynasty collapsed in 220, China was split into several competing kingdoms, each ruled by military leaders. This time is called the Period of Disunion. The era lasted for more than 350 years, from 220 to 589. During this period, nomadic tribes settled in northern China, and many northern Chinese moved south. These movements resulted in blended cultures in both north and south China.

> What were the two general elements in the blended culture of northern China during the Period of Disunion?
> _____
> _____
> _____

THE SUI, TANG, AND SONG

After this time of political confusion and cultural change, China was reunified. Under the Sui, Tang, and Song dynasties, China remained unified for most of the next 700 years.

The Sui (SWAY) dynasty was established by a northern leader called Yang Chien (YANG jee-en). In 589 he led his army to conquer lands to the west and south and reunified China. The Tang dynasty replaced the Sui in 618. The Tang ruled China for nearly 300 years. During this period, Chinese power and influence reached all of east and Southeast Asia, as well as much of Central Asia.

> Who was the first Sui ruler?
> _____
> _____

> How many years did the Sui dynasty last?
> _____
> _____

Historians view the Tang dynasty as a golden age of Chinese civilization. Among its leaders, three are especially notable. Taizong (TY-tzoong) conquered most of Central Asia, reformed the military, and created law codes. In the reign of Xuanzong (SHOO-AN-tzoong), culture flourished and many of China's finest poets wrote. **Empress Wu**, the only woman to rule China, ruled with an iron first, but she but kept China stable and prosperous.

> **Name three important Tang rulers.**
> _____
> _____
> _____

After the Tang dynasty fell, China entered a period of 53 years known as Five Dynasties and Ten Kingdoms. Then, in 960, China was again reunified under the Song dynasty, and another great period of accomplishment began that lasted for about 300 years, until 1279.

THE AGE OF BUDDHISM

During the troubled Period of Disunion, many Chinese people turned to Buddhism. They took comfort in the Buddhist teaching that people can escape suffering and achieve a state of peace. During the Sui and Tang dynasties, Buddhism became well established throughout China and Buddhist temples arose across the land.

> **Why do you think Buddhism comforted people during the Period of Disunion?**
> _____
> _____
> _____
> _____

Buddhism influenced many aspects of Chinese culture, including art, literature, and architecture. Chinese Buddhist missionaries brought the religion to Japan, Korea, and other Asian lands. Despite a Tang emperor's campaign against the religion, Buddhism remained a vital part of Chinese culture.

CHALLENGE ACTIVITY

Critical Thinking: Sequence Research the origin and development of Buddhism before it became popular in China. **HSS Analysis Skills HR 1, HI 1, HI 2, HI 3**

China

MAIN IDEAS

1. Advances in agriculture led to increased trade and population growth.

2. Cities and trade grew during the Tang and Song dynasties

3. The Tang and Song dynasties produced fine arts and inventions.

 HSS 7.3
Students analyze the geographic, political, economic, religious, and social structures of the civilizations of China of the Middle Ages.

Key Terms and People

porcelain a thin, beautiful pottery invented by the Chinese

gunpowder a mixture of powders used in guns and explosives

compass an instrument that uses the earth's magnetic field to indicate direction

woodblock printing a form of printing in which an entire page is carved into a block of wood that is covered with ink and then pressed against paper to make a copy of the page

Section Summary

ADVANCES IN AGRICULTURE

Under the Song dynasty, Chinese agriculture reached new heights. Farmers created elaborate irrigation systems based on new techniques and devices. The amount of land under cultivation increased. Farmers developed a new type of fast-ripening rice that enabled them to grow two or even three crops in the time it used to take to grow just one. They also learned to grow cotton efficently and processed the fiber to make clothes and other goods.

Merchants traded food crops, so food was abundant not just in the countryside but in the cities, too. Population grew to more than 100 million people, making China the most populous country in the world.

What was the advantage of fast-ripening rice?

_____

_____

_____

Do you think agricultural abundance and the growth of cities are connected? Why?

_____

_____

_____

_____

CITIES AND TRADE

Chinese cities grew and flourished as the trade centers of the Tang and Song dynasties. Chang'an (chahng-AHN), with a population of more than a million people, was by far the largest city in the world at the time. Traders used the Grand Canal, a series of waterways that linked major cities, to ship goods and agricultural products throughout China.

Foreign trade used both land routes and sea routes. China's Pacific ports were open to foreign traders. A bustling trade was carried on with India, Africa, and Southwest Asia. Chinese exports included tea, rice, spices, and jade. Especially prized by foreigners, however, were silk and **porcelain**. The methods of making these Chinese inventions were kept secret for centuries.

> **Why do you think the Chinese did not want foreigners to know how to make silk and porcelain?**
>
> _____
> _____
> _____
> _____

ARTS AND INVENTIONS

The Tang dynasty produced some of China's greatest artists and writers, including Li Po and Du Fu—the most famous of all Chinese poets—and the Buddhist painter Wu Daozi (DOW-tzee). The Song dynasty produced Li Qingzhao (ching-ZHOW), perhaps China's greatest female poet. Artists of both dynasties created exquisite objects in clay, particularly porcelain items with a pale green glaze called celadon (SEL-uh-duhn).

> **Use the Internet or a library to find a poem by Li Po.**

The Tang and Song dynasties produced some of the most remarkable—and important—inventions in human history, including **gunpowder** and the **compass**.

The world's oldest-known printed book, using **woodblock printing**, was printed in China in 868. Later, during the Song dynasty, the Chinese invented movable type for printing. The Song dynasty also introduced the concept of paper money.

> **What printing technology ultimately superseded woodblock printing?**
>
> _____
> _____

CHALLENGE ACTIVITY

Critical Thinking: Drawing Inferences Create a document showing an exchange of goods between a Song dynasty Chinese trader and a foreign merchant. **HSS Analysis Skills HR 3, HI 1, HI 6**

China

MAIN IDEAS

1. Confucianism underwent changes and influenced Chinese government.
2. Scholar-officials ran China's government during the Song dynasty.

 HSS 7.3
Students analyze the geographic, political, economic, religious, and social structures of the civilizations of China of the Middle Ages.

Key Terms and People

bureaucracy body of unelected government officials
civil service service as a government official
scholar-official an educated member of the government

Academic Vocabulary

function work or perform
incentive something that leads people to follow a certain course of action

Section Summary

CONFUCIANISM

Confucianism is the name given to the ideas of the Chinese philosopher Confucius. Confucius's teachings focused on ethics, or proper behavior, of individuals and governments. He argued that society would **function** best if everyone followed two principles, *ren* and *li*. *Ren* means concern for others, and *li* means following appropriate customs and behavior. Order in society is maintained when people know their place and behave appropriately.

> Conduct some research to find the title usually given in English to a book containing Confucius's ideas. Write that title here.
> _____
> _____

For a thousand years after his death, Confucius's ideas went in and out of favor several times. Early in the Song dynasty, however, a new version of Confucianism, known as neo-Confucianism, was adopted as official government policy. In addition to teaching proper behavior, neo-Confucian scholars and officials discussed spiritual questions like what made human beings do bad things even if their basic nature was good.

> Before the Song dynasty, what religious belief probably had a negative effect on the popularity of Confucianism in China?
> _____
> _____

SCHOLAR-OFFICIALS

The Song dynasty took another major step that would affect the Chinese imperial state for centuries to come. The Song established a system by which people went to work for the government. These workers formed a large **bureaucracy** by passing a series of written **civil service** examinations.

The tests covered both the traditional teachings of Confucius and spiritual questions. Because the tests were extremely difficult, students spent years preparing for them. Often only very few students passed the exam. Candidates had a strong **incentive** for studying hard. Passing the tests meant life as a **scholar-official**, whose benefits included considerable respect, a good salary, and reduced penalties for breaking the law.

The civil service examination system helped ensure that talented, intelligent people became scholar-officials. This system was a major factor in the stability of the Song government.

> Name a well-known government today that has a large bureaucracy.
> _____
> _____

> Draw a picture of what you think a Song scholar-official might look like.

CHALLENGE ACTIVITY

Critical Thinking: Drawing Inferences Write a short essay on the relation between the Song dynasty development of civil service and the Confucian ideals of *ren* and *li*. **HSS Analysis Skills CS 1, HI 1, HI 2, HI 3**

China

MAIN IDEAS

1. The Mongol Empire included China, and the Mongols ruled China as the Yuan dynasty.
2. The Ming dynasty was a time of stability and prosperity.
3. China under the Ming saw great changes in its government and relations with other countries.

 HSS 7.3
Students analyze the geographic, political, economic, religious, and social structures of the civilizations of China of the Middle Ages.

Key Terms and People

Genghis Khan powerful leader who united the Mongols

Kublai Khan Genghis Khan's grandson, who completed the conquest of China

Zheng He famous seafaring voyager of the Ming dynasty

isolationism a policy of removing a country from contact with other countries

Academic Vocabulary

consequences effects of a particular event or events

Section Summary

THE MONGOL EMPIRE

For centuries, the Mongols had lived as nomadic tribes in the vast plains north of China. Then in 1206, a powerful leader known as **Genghis Khan** (jeng-giz KAHN) united them. He led huge armies on bloody expeditions of conquest throughout much of Asia and Eastern Europe.

Genghis Khan first led his armies into northern China in 1211. They fought their way south, wrecking whole towns and ruining farmland. By the time of Genghis Khan's death in 1227, all of northern China was under Mongol control.

Genghis Khan's grandson, **Kublai Khan** (KOO-bluh KAHN), completed the conquest of China and declared himself emperor of China in 1279. He named his new dynasty the Yuan dynasty. Kublai

> **What country today represents the homeland of the Mongols?**
>
> _____
>
> _____

> **How many years did it take for the Mongol armies to conquer all of China?**
>
> _____
>
> _____

Interactive Reader and Study Guide

Section 4, *continued*

Khan's empire, which stretched all the way to eastern Europe, covered more land than any other empire in world history.

Kublai Khan's regime preserved much of the structure of the Song dynasty, including the civil service and trade routes. The Italian merchant Marco Polo, who traveled in China between 1271 and 1295, wrote of a highly civilized country and sparked Europeans' interest in China.

> **Which two aspects of Song civilization would you say Kublai Khan appreciated the most?**
> _____
> _____
> _____

Two failed campaigns against Japan and expensive public works projects gradually weakened the Yuan dynasty. Many Chinese groups rebelled. Finally, in 1368, Chu Yuan-Chang (JOO yoo-ahn-JAHNG) took control and founded the Ming dynasty.

THE MING DYNASTY

The Ming dynasty lasted nearly 300 years, from 1368 to 1644. Ming China proved to be one of the most stable and prosperous times in Chinese history. Great Ming achievements include the fabulous ships and goodwill voyages of **Zheng He** (juhng HUH), the famous Forbidden City at the center of Beijing, and the Great Wall of China.

> **What do you think was the original reason for building the Great Wall?**
> _____
> _____
> _____
> _____

CHINA UNDER THE MING

Around 1400 China's emperor and scholar-officials began to react against the popular influence of foreign goods, beliefs, and customs, and the increasing wealth and power of merchants. China entered a period of **isolationism**. Ironically, the **consequences** of this policy included a weakness that allowed opportunistic Westerners to seize considerable power in some parts of China as China's imperial glory faded.

> **Name another major country whose history includes a period of isolationism.**
> _____
> _____

CHALLENGE ACTIVITY

Critical Thinking: Drawing Inferences Draw a street map of an imaginary city. Include a "forbidden city" within it that is restricted to a certain group of your choosing. **HSS Analysis Skills CS 3, HI 2**

Japan

CHAPTER SUMMARY

Cause	→	Effect
	→	The first Japanese rulers
Prince Shotoku's reign	→	
The emperor's move to Heian court	→	Daimyos hiring shoguns and samurai for protection

COMPREHENSION AND CRITICAL THINKING

Use the answers to the following questions to fill in the graphic organizer above.

1. Explain Who were the first rulers of Japan and how did they get to be rulers?

_____

_____

2. Identify Cause and Effect How did Prince Shotoku's interest in all things Chinese impact Japanese culture?

_____

_____

3. Evaluate Why were the Japanese willing to submit to shogun and samurai rule?

_____

_____

4. Draw a Conclusion Why do you think the shogun kept the emperor in place as a figurehead, even though the emperor was a ruler with no power?

_____

_____

_____

Japan

MAIN IDEAS

1. Geography shaped life in Japan.
2. Early Japanese society was organized in clans, which came to be ruled by an emperor.
3. Japan learned about language, society, and government from China and Korea.

 HSS 7.5
Students analyze the geographic, political, economic, religious, and social structures of the civilizations of Medieval Japan.

Key Terms and People

clans extended families

Shinto the traditional religion of Japan, based on the belief that everything in nature has a spirit

Prince Shotoku popular Japanese ruler who brought many Chinese ideas to Japan

regent someone who rules for someone who is unable rule alone

Section Summary

GEOGRAPHY SHAPES LIFE IN JAPAN

The islands of Japan are the tops of undersea mountains and volcanoes. Because it is difficult to live and farm on mountain slopes, most Japanese people have always lived in the few flat areas along the coastal plains.

The nearness of the sea means that seafood has been a key part of the Japanese diet for thousands of years. Isolation has contributed to a distinctive Japanese culture, although the Japanese have been influenced by nearby Korea and China.

EARLY JAPANESE SOCIETY

Early Japan was home to two different cultures, neither of which had much—if any—contact with the rest of Asia. The Ainu (EYE-noo), with a look and language distinct from the rest of Asia, were driven by conflict to the northern island of Hokkaido. Over time, the Ainu culture almost disappeared.

> **Why is most of Japan's land hilly, and not flat?**
> _____
> _____
> _____
> _____

> **What geographic feature is probably the main reason why Japan's early culture was so distinct from that of other parts of Asia?**
> _____
> _____
> _____

Interactive Reader and Study Guide

Section 1, *continued*

The people living to the south of the Ainu eventually became the Japanese. They lived mostly in small farm villages. **Clans**, or extended families, ruled these villages. They practiced religious rituals that became **Shinto**, the traditional religion of Japan. According to this tradition, everything in nature has a spirit, or *kami* (KAH-mee).

Some clans became so powerful that they took over much of Japan. The Yamato rulers were the first clan to call themselves emperors of Japan.

> What was the unit of political life in early Japan?
>
> _____
>
> _____

JAPAN LEARNS FROM CHINA AND KOREA

By the mid-500s, Japanese rulers yearned to learn new things. They sent emissaries to Korea and China to learn about those cultures. Chinese culture was very influential in Japan. With no written language of their own, the Japanese used Chinese characters to spell out Japanese sounds and words. Chinese was actually Japan's official language from about 500 to about 1100.

> For about how many centuries was Chinese the official language of Japan?
>
> _____
>
> _____

Prince Shotoku (shoh-toh-koo), who served as **regent** for his aunt the empress, was a major proponent of Chinese culture. Shotoku had advisors introduce the Chinese philosophy of Confucianism to Japan. He also encouraged the spread of Buddhism. Shotoku's attempt to bring a more absolute, Chinese-style of rule to Japan did not fare as well. Clan leaders opposed it. They were afraid to give up their power. Prince Shotoku died without achieving his goals. Later rulers put many of his ideas in practice, though.

> Underline the sentence that explains why the clan leaders did not want a Chinese-style rule.

CHALLENGE ACTIVITY

Critical Thinking: Drawing Inferences Why do you think the Japanese were so interested in learning from the Chinese and the Koreans? Write a one-page essay describing specific examples of what China and other cultures offered that Japan did not have at the time. **HSS Analysis Skills HI 1, HI 5**

Japan

MAIN IDEAS
1. Japanese nobles created great art in their court at Heian.
2. Buddhism changed in Japan during the Heian period.

 HSS 7.5
Students analyze the geographic, political, economic, religious, and social structures of the civilizations of Medieval Japan.

Key Terms and People

court group of nobles who serve as advisors to a ruler

Lady Murasaki Shikibu Japanese writer credited with writing the world's first novel

Zen form of Buddhism involving quiet, thoughtful meditation

Section Summary

JAPANESE NOBLES CREATE GREAT ART

In 794 the emperor and empress of Japan moved to Heian (HAY-ahn), a city now called Kyoto. The nobles who followed created an imperial **court**. These nobles had little to do with the common people of Heian. They lived apart from poorer citizens and seldom left the city. They loved beauty and made the court at Heian the center of a golden age of art and learning between 794 and 1185.

These nobles dressed in beautiful silk robes and carried decorative fans. They were also lovers of the written and spoken word, and spent many hours writing in journals. Several women of the Heian court wrote in the Japanese language, although Chinese was the official language. As a result, women wrote most of the major works of early Japanese literature.

Probably the greatest of these early writers was **Lady Murasaki Shikibu** (moohr-ah-sahk-ee shee-kee-boo). Around 1000, she wrote *The Tale of Genji*, often considered the world's first full-length novel. It is the story of a prince named Genji and his quest for love. During his search he meets women from many different social classes.

> **Why do you think the nobles of Heian devoted so much time to the promotion of the arts?**
> _____
> _____
> _____
> _____

> **Circle the name of the author of what is considered the world's first novel.**

Visual arts were also popular, particularly painting, calligraphy, and architecture. The paintings were made in bright, bold colors. Most Heian architecture was based on that of the Chinese capital. Other architectural styles were simple and airy. Wood houses with tiled roofs featured large open spaces surrounded by elegant gardens. Performing arts also flourished at the Heian court, particularly a form of drama called Noh, which combined music, dance and speaking parts. Noh plays often presented the feats of great Japanese heroes.

> **What class of people do you think provided food and services for the Heian court?**
> _____
> _____

BUDDHISM CHANGES

Common Japanese people had no time for the long, elaborate rituals practiced by the court. Both groups were deeply religious, however. The Japanese introduced important changes to the Buddhism, which had been brought from China. Some new forms of Buddhism blended elements of Shinto Other forms were unique to Japan. One very popular form, called Pure Land Buddhism, did not require any special rituals. Instead, Pure Land Buddhists chanted the Buddha's name over and over again.

> **What did Pure Land Buddhism require of its followers?**
> _____
> _____
> _____

In the 1100s a new form of Buddhism called **Zen** developed. Zen Buddhists believed that neither faith nor good behavior led to wisdom. Instead, people should practice self-discipline and meditation, or quiet thinking. These ideas appealed to many Japanese, especially warriors. As these warriors gained more influence in Japan, so did Zen Buddhism.

> **Underline the phrase that defines the central practices of Zen Buddhism.**

CHALLENGE ACTIVITY

Critical Thinking: Drawing Inferences If you were a noble in the Heian court who did not have to work, what would you do all day? Write a journal entry in the style and manner of a Japanese noble, describing a typical day. **HSS Analysis Skills CR 4, HI 3**

Japan

MAIN IDEAS

1. Samurai and shoguns took over Japan as emperors lost influence.

2. Samurai warriors lived honorably.

3. Order broke down when the power of the shoguns was challenged by invaders and rebellions.

4. Strong leaders took over and reunified Japan.

 HSS 7.5

Students analyze the geographic, political, economic, religious, and social structures of the civilizations of Medieval Japan.

Key Terms and People

daimyo large landowner

samurai trained professional warriors

figurehead a person who appears to rule though real power rests with someone else

shogun a general who ruled Japan in the emperor's name

Bushido the strict samurai code of rules

Section Summary

SAMURAI AND SHOGUNS TAKE OVER JAPAN

While the Heian court flourished, order was breaking down in Japanese society. By the late 1100s, powerful nobles were openly at war. Rebels fought against imperial officials. Japan's rulers did not notice the problems growing in their country.

Japan's large landowners, or **daimyo** (DY-mee-oh), decided they could not rely on the emperor to protect them. They hired **samurai** (SA-muh-ry), trained professional warriors, to defend their property. Several noble clans decided to seize power themselves.

Two of these clans fought each other fiercely for 30 years. Finally, the head of the Minamoto clan declared himself Japan's new ruler. The Minamoto leader kept the emperor on as a **figurehead**. The Minamoto leader took the title **shogun**. He ruled in

> Underline the phrase that explains why the daimyo went out and hired their own protection in the late 1100s.

> To what clan did Japan's first shogun belong?
> _____
> _____

the emperor's name. When he died, he passed his
title and power on to one of his children. For about
the next 700 years, Japan was ruled by shoguns.

> Circle how many years the shoguns would rule Japan.

SAMURAI LIVE HONORABLY

The samurai enjoyed many privileges, but also
had to follow a strict code of rules called **Bushido**
(booh-shi-doh). Loyalty and honor were central to
this code. Both men and women of samurai families
learned to fight.

ORDER BREAKS DOWN

The shoguns, with the help of the samurai, kept
order in Japan for nearly a century. Slowly that
order broke down. Two foreign invasions by the
Mongols were stopped, but the authority of the
shoguns weakened. Increasingly, nobles began to
resent the shoguns' power over them. The daimyo
and the emperor worked together to limit the power
of the shogun.

> Why do you think the emperor might resent the power of the shoguns?
> _____
> _____
> _____
> _____

STRONG LEADERS TAKE OVER

Eventually, new leaders rose to power. Each fought
to unify all of Japan under his control. The first to
restore the power of the shogun was Oda Nobunaga
(ohd-ah noh-booh-nah-gah), who ruled half of
Japan by 1582. Other shoguns who followed
stabilized Japanese rule. The shogun Tokugawa
Ieyasu (toh-koohg-ah-wuh ee-e-yahs-ooh) sent
emissaries out to the world. Others, however, feared
the intrusion of foreigners. In 1630, the reigning
shogun closed off Japan completely. This extended
the samurai period until the 1800s.

> Which shogun opened Japan up the world?
> _____
> _____

CHALLENGE ACTIVITY

Critical Thinking: Drawing Inferences You are an ordinary Japanese
citizen living in the Middle Ages. To whom do you pledge the highest
allegiance—the gods, the emperor, the shogun, or the samurai who
work for them? Explain your reasoning in a one-page essay. **HSS
Analysis Skills CR 5, HI 1.**

Interactive Reader and Study Guide

The Early Middle Ages

> **HISTORY–SOCIAL SCIENCE STANDARDS**
> HSS 7.6 Students analyze the geographic, political, economic, religious, and social structures of the civilizations of Medieval Europe.

CHAPTER SUMMARY

The need for lords to protect their land	led to	
	led to	**knights maintaining an honorable code of behavior**
Feudalism	led to	**people's lives bound together by honor and duty**
Self-sufficient manors	led to	

COMPREHENSION AND CRITICAL THINKING

Use the answers to the following questions to fill in the graphic organizer above.

1. Explain How did the lord of a manor protect his land?

_____

_____

2. Identify Cause and Effect What kept a knight from abusing his power?

_____

_____

3. Evaluate How did an economic system of land and service, rather than money, impact people's lives?

_____

_____

4. Draw a Conclusion How was manor life different than town and city life?

_____

_____

The Early Middle Ages

MAIN IDEAS

1. The physical features of Europe vary widely from region to region.
2. Geography has shaped life in Europe, including where and how people live.

 HSS 7.6
Students analyze the geographic, political, economic, religious, and social structures of the civilizations of Medieval Europe.

Key Terms and People

Eurasia the large landmass that includes Europe and Asia

topography the shape and elevation of the land in a region

Section Summary

THE PHYSICAL FEATURES OF EUROPE

Europe is a small continent, but it is very diverse. Many different landforms, water features, and climates can be found there. Although we call Europe a continent, it is part of **Eurasia**, a large landmass that includes both Europe and Asia.

Europe's **topography**, the shape and elevation of the land, varies widely from place to place. Southern Europe is very mountainous, with some of the world's highest mountains in the Alps. As you travel north, the land gets flat. Northern Europe was once covered in thick forests.

Most of Europe's rivers are in the north. Farther north, the land gets rugged and hilly again, though not as high as the mountains in the south. Many peninsulas jut out from Europe, creating a long and jagged coastline. The climate is hotter and drier in the south, and gets progressively colder as you move north.

GEOGRAPHY SHAPES LIFE

Not surprisingly, with this variety of topography and climate, life in early Europe was different depending upon where you lived. In southern Europe, most people lived on coastal plains or in river valleys where the land was flat enough to farm.

> **Why is Europe considered to be part of Eurasia?**
> _____
> _____
> _____

> **What is the highest mountain range in Europe?**
> _____
> _____

Name _____ Class _____ Date _____

Section 1, *continued*

People grew crops like grapes and olives that could grow on mountainsides and also survive the region's dry summers. High in the mountains, where the land was too steep or rocky to farm, people raised sheep and goats.

Because southern Europe has a long coastline with numerous peninsulas, many people turned to the sea for food and transportation. Societies that lived in southern Europe often became great traders and seafarers.

Most people in northern Europe lived much farther from the sea than people in southern Europe did. They still had access to the sea, however, through northern Europe's many rivers. Because rivers were an easy means of transportation, many towns grew up along them. These rivers also sometimes provided protection for cities.

In the fields around cities, farmers took advantage of northern Europe's rich soils to grow all sorts of crops. These fields were excellent farmlands, but the flat land also created an easy route for invaders to follow. No mountains blocked people's access to northern Europe. As a result, the region was frequently invaded.

> List two reasons why grapes and olives are ideal crops for southern Europe.
> _____
> _____
> _____
> _____

> List two reasons why Northern Europe was frequently invaded.
> _____
> _____
> _____
> _____

CHALLENGE ACTIVITY

Critical Thinking: Drawing Inferences Where would you have preferred to live in Europe during the Middle Ages, if you had your choice? Write a short letter to a family member explaining what daily life is like in the area you choose and why you like it there. **HSS Analysis Skills HI 1, HI 6**

Interactive Reader and Study Guide

The Early Middle Ages

MAIN IDEAS

1. Christianity spread to northern Europe through the work of missionaries and monks.

2. The Franks, led by Charlemagne, created a huge Christian empire and brought together scholars from around Europe.

3. Invaders threatened much of Europe in the 700s and 800s.

 HSS 7.6
Students analyze the geographic, political, economic, religious, and social structures of the civilizations of Medieval Europe.

Key Terms and People

Middle Ages the period lasting from about 500 to about 1500

medieval another name for the Middle Ages

Saint Patrick Christian missionary credited with converting Ireland to Christianity

monks religious men who lived apart from society in isolated communities

monasteries communities of monks

Saint Benedict monk responsible for creating the Benedictine rule, a code prescribing a monk's behavior

Charlemagne warrior and king who led the Franks in building a huge empire

Section Summary

CHRISTIANITY SPREADS TO NORTHERN EUROPE

Europe was a dangerous place during Rome's long collapse. Without the Roman government, Europe had no central authority to keep order. Various groups from the north and east moved into former Roman lands, creating their own states and making their own kings. These kings often fought among themselves. As a result, by the early 500s Europe was divided into many small kingdoms. This marked the beginning of the **Middle Ages**, or **medieval** period.

At the beginning of the Middle Ages, most of the kingdoms of northern Europe were not Christian. Christianity was common only in places that had been part of the Roman Empire, such as Italy and

> List three reasons why Europe was so dangerous around the year 500.
>
> _____
>
> _____
>
> _____

> Why is the period between about 500 and about 1500 called the Middle Ages?
>
> _____
>
> _____

Section 2, *continued*

Spain. As time passed, Christianity slowly spread
farther north, largely through the efforts of two
groups of Christians—monks and missionaries.

The pope sent missionaries to northern Europe,
hoping that Christianity would make Europe a safer
place. Missionaries converted much of Germany,
France, and Britain. One of the earliest missionaries,
Saint Patrick, was an English Christian who took it
upon himself to convert Ireland. Unlike missionaries
monks lived apart from society in isolated
communities, praying, working, and meditating.
Communities of monks, or **monasteries**, were built
all over Europe in the Middle Ages. Most monks
followed a strict set of rules created in the early 500s
by **Saint Benedict**.

> **Did the pope send Saint Patrick to Ireland?**
> _____
> _____

THE FRANKS BUILD AN EMPIRE

In the 500s a powerful group called the Franks
conquered Gaul, the region we now call France.
Under a ruler named Clovis, the Franks became
Christian and created one of the strongest
kingdoms in Europe. The Franks reached their
greatest power during the 700s under **Charlemagne**
(SHAHR-luh-mayn). At its height Charlemagne's
empire reached from France into modern Germany,
Austria, Italy, and northern Spain. Religious
scholarship flourished in Charlemagne's time.

> **Who established Christianity among the Franks?**
> _____
> _____

INVADERS THREATEN EUROPE

While Charlemagne was building his empire,
Europe was being attacked on all sides by invaders.
The most fearsome were the swift and vicious
attacks of the Vikings from Scandinavia.

> **Why do you think the Vikings are still so vividly remembered in our culture today?**
> _____
> _____
> _____
> _____

CHALLENGE ACTIVITY

Critical Thinking: Drawing Inferences The life of a monk in the Middle
Ages was strict and without luxuries. Why would someone want to
become a monk? Write a letter from the point of view of someone who
wishes to join a monastery, explaining your decision to live the life of a
monk. **HSS Analysis Skills CR 1, HI 1**

The Early Middle Ages

Section 3

┌───┐
MAIN IDEAS

1. Feudalism governed how knights and nobles dealt with each other.
2. Feudalism spread through much of Europe.
3. The manor system dominated Europe's economy.
4. Towns and trade grew and helped end the feudal system.
└───┘

 HSS 7.6
Students analyze the geographic, political, economic, religious, and social structures of the civilizations of Medieval Europe.

Key Terms and People

knights warriors who fought on horseback

vassal a knight who agrees to protect and serve a lord in exchange for land

feudalism the system that governs the relationship between lords and vassals

William the Conqueror French noble who conquered England and spread feudalism

manor large estate owned by a knight or lord

serfs workers who were tied to the land on which they lived

Eleanor of Aquitaine powerful French noblewoman who became queen of France and England

Section Summary

FEUDALISM GOVERNS KNIGHTS AND NOBLES

After Charlemagne's time, raids on Europe from the north and east intensified. The Frankish kings were unable to defend their empire. Nobles had to defend their own lands. Many nobles began to rule their lands as independent territories. These nobles needed soldiers. They gave **knights**, warriors who fought on horseback, land in exchange for military service. A noble who gave land to a knight was called a lord, while the knight was called a **vassal**. The system that governed the promises between lords and vassals is called **feudalism**.

Lords and vassals had responsibilities to each other. A lord had to send help if an enemy attacked a vassal. A lord had to be fair or vassals could break

┌─────────────────────────────┐
Why did many nobles become rulers of their own lands?

_____

_____

_____
└─────────────────────────────┘

Name _____ Class _____ Date _____

Section 3, *continued*

all ties with him. Vassals had to fight at a lord's command. They also had to house and feed a lord if he visited and sometimes pay him money.

List two responsibilities of a vassal toward a lord.

_____
_____
_____

FEUDALISM SPREADS

Frankish knights introduced feudalism into northern Italy, Spain, and Germany. From Germany, knights carried feudalism into eastern Europe. Feudalism reached Britain when **William the Conqueror** invaded and made himself king of England.

Who brought feudalism to eastern Europe?

_____
_____

THE MANOR SYSTEM

An estate owned by a knight or lord was called a **manor**. As fighters, knights had no time to work in the fields. Most peasants owned no land but needed to grow food to live. So knights allowed peasants to live and farm land on their estates. In return the peasants, or **serfs**, had to give the knights food or other payment. Skilled craftsman also lived and worked on the manor, which provided everything people needed.

What group supported the work of skilled craftsmen under feudalism?

_____
_____

Women in the Middle Ages had fewer rights than men, but they still played important roles in society. Some women, like **Eleanor of Aquitaine**, even became politically powerful.

TOWNS AND TRADE GROW

Most people lived in manors during the Middle Ages, but as Europe's population grew so did the size and number of towns and cities. The invention of the plough and increased trade eventually led to the decline of feudalism as people had more opportunities to make a living.

Why do you think people left the manors for the towns and cities?

_____
_____
_____
_____

CHALLENGE ACTIVITY

Critical Thinking: Drawing Inferences During the Middle Ages the ability for a person to better their lot depended upon where they started out in life. Research the options for advancement for the following people: the lord of the manor, lady of the manor, a vassal, a peasant, and a serf. **HSS Analysis Skills CR 1, HI 1, HI 5**

Interactive Reader and Study Guide

The Early Middle Ages

Section 4

MAIN IDEAS

1. Feudal societies shared common elements in Europe and Japan.
2. Europe and Japan differed in their cultural elements such as religion and art.

 HSS 7.6
Students analyze the geographic, political, economic, religious, and social structures of the civilizations of Medieval Europe.

Key Terms and People

chivalry code of honorable behavior for European knights

haiku short poems, with only three lines and 17 syllables, that usually describe nature themes

Section Summary

FEUDAL SOCIETIES SHARE COMMON ELEMENTS

Feudalism was not unique to Europe. You may have noticed a connection between the lords and vassals of Europe and, half a world away, the samurai and the daimyo of Japan. But how similar were the two societies?

Both knights and samurai were paid in land, rather than in money, and had peasants work the land for them. Both collected part of the crop yield in return for allowing the peasants to farm on their property. Both kinds of warriors promised to serve and fight for their nobles. In exchange for the land, both lords and daimyo expected their warriors to behave with honor and loyalty. The Japanese code of behavior for a samurai was called Bushido. A similar code of honorable behavior for European knights was called **chivalry**.

> **How were knights, or vassals, and samurai paid for their military service?**
>
> _____
>
> _____

> **Underline the names of the two codes of honor that ruled behavior for the knights and samurai.**

EUROPE AND JAPAN DIFFER

Still, there were many differences between the two cultures. Perhaps the main difference was expressed through religion. Although religion was important to both groups, the religious concepts were different. The Europeans were mostly Christians, while the Japanese had blended the naturalistic Shinto religion, where everything has a spirit, with Buddhism and Confucianism. Religion strongly influences the way people look at life and ultimately how they act.

The differences in religion appear in the art of the two cultures. In Europe most art of the Middle Ages showed Christian religious themes. Painting and sculpture represented scenes from the Bible or male and female saints. Poems and stories often taught people how to live or tried to inspire them with the lives of great Christians.

> **What is the main subject of most European medieval art?**
> _____
> _____

The art of Japan, on the other hand, expressed mostly natural scenes. Paintings of nature were common, and people designed and built beautiful gardens. The simple wooden architecture of a house was designed to blend into nature, rather than stand out. Japanese literature also celebrated nature. For example, Japanese poets in the 1600s created **haiku**, short poems of three lines and 17 syllables that often describe scenes of nature.

> **Write a haiku.**
> _____
> _____
> _____
> _____

Still, it is remarkable that similar systems of feudalism developed at the same time in two completely different cultures, located so far from each other. While feudalism has faded, it still impacts the life and culture of these two different regions today.

CHALLENGE ACTIVITY

Critical Thinking: Drawing Inferences How do you think religion influences your modern outlook and the people around you? Think hard about this concept. Even if you do not hold religious beliefs yourself, religion is a system of thought that influences how you view life and how you act. Write a brief essay discussing how your thoughts and attitudes on religion reflect the way you view the world. **HSS Analysis Skills HI 2, HI 3**

The Later Middle Ages

HISTORY–SOCIAL SCIENCE STANDARDS
HSS 7.6 Students analyze the geographic, political, economic, religious, and social structures of the civilizations of Medieval Europe.
HSS Analysis Skill CS 3 Identify physical and cultural features.
HSS Analysis Skill HI 2 Understand and distinguish cause and effect.

CHAPTER SUMMARY

The rise of Christianity	led to	**an increase in the political power of the church.**
The Black Death	led to	**the demise of the manor system.**
The Magna Carta	led to	**a new set of rights founding modern democracy.**
Challenges to church authority	led to	**persecution of Jews and other non-Christians.**

COMPREHENSION AND CRITICAL THINKING

Use information from the graphic organizer and from the following pages to answer the following questions.

1. **Explain** Name one reason why the church became more politically powerful in the Later Middle Ages?

_____

2. **Identify Cause and Effect** How did the Black Death cause the end of the manor system?

_____

3. **Evaluate** Who wrote the Magna Carta? Why is it important to history?

_____

_____

4. **Draw a Conclusion** Why do you think the rise of Christianity led to increased intolerance of Jews and other non-Christians?

_____

_____

The Later Middle Ages

Section 1

MAIN IDEAS

1. Popes and kings ruled Europe as spiritual and political leaders.
2. Popes fought for power, leading to a permanent split within the church.
3. Kings and popes clashed over some issues.

 HSS 7.6
Students analyze the geographic, political, economic, religious, and social structures of the civilizations of Medieval Europe.

Key Terms and People

excommunicate casting an offender out of the church
Pope Gregory VII pope who excommunicated Emperor Henry IV
Emperor Henry IV Holy Roman ruler who challenged Pope Gregory VII

Section Summary

POPES AND KINGS RULE EUROPE

In the early Middle Ages, great nobles and their knights held most of the political power. As time passed this power began to shift to two types of leaders, popes and kings. The pope had great spiritual power. The kings had political power. Together, the pope and the kings controlled most of European society.

The pope was the head of the Christian Church. Since nearly everyone in the Middle Ages belonged to this church, the pope had great power. Christians believed that the pope was God's representative on earth. Because the pope was seen as God's representative, it was his duty to decide what the church would teach. From time to time, a pope would write a letter called a bull to explain a religious teaching or outline a church policy.

It was also the pope's duty to decide when someone was acting against the church. For the most serious offenses, the pope could choose to **excommunicate**, or cast out, an offender from the church. This much power often put the pope in direct conflict with the kings.

> **Name two of the pope's responsibilities as leader of the Christian church.**
> _____
> _____
> _____
> _____

> **Why do you think people feared the pope's ability to excommunicate them?**
> _____
> _____
> _____
> _____

Interactive Reader and Study Guide

Section 1, *continued*

In 1000 Europe was divided into many states that were ruled by kings. Many of the kings did not have much power. But the kings of England, France, and the Holy Roman Empire held a lot of power. In France and England, the throne was inherited through family. The Holy Roman Empire got its name because the empire existed with the pope's approval. In the Holy Roman Empire, the nobles elected the emperor. The pope settled any disagreements among the nobles.

> Underline how emperors were selected in France and England. Now, circle how an emperor was selected in the Holy Roman Empire.

POPES FIGHT FOR POWER

The popes of Western Europe tried to assert their authority over the bishops of Eastern Europe. The bishops of Eastern Europe did not want to answer to the pope. Pope Leo IX excommunicated the bishop of Constantinople when the bishop would not recognize the pope's authority. This caused a permanent split in the church between the Eastern Orthodox Church and the Roman Catholic Church.

> What event caused a permanent split in the church?
> _____
> _____
> _____
> _____

KINGS AND POPES CLASH

Popes also argued with kings, particularly over the king's right to select bishops. A dispute arose when **Pope Gregory VII** did not like a bishop chosen by Holy Roman Emperor **Henry IV**. Henry tried to remove the pope from office. The pope excommunicated Henry. Henry had to beg for the pope's forgiveness to remain in power. After their deaths, a compromise was ultimately struck. From then on, the pope would select religious officials, but religious officals must obey the emperor.

> During the lifetimes of Gregory and Henry, who would you say won their battle of wills?
> _____
> _____

CHALLENGE ACTIVITY

Critical Thinking: Drawing Inferences Would you have rather been a pope or a king during the Middle Ages? Write a one-page paper defending your answer. **HSS Analysis Skills, CR 4, HI 1**

Interactive Reader and Study Guide

The Later Middle Ages

Section 2

MAIN IDEAS

1. The pope called on Crusaders to invade the Holy Land.
2. Despite some initial success, the later Crusades failed.
3. The Crusades changed Europe forever.

 HSS 7.6
Students analyze the geographic, political, economic, religious, and social structures of the civilizations of Medieval Europe.

Key Terms and People

Crusades a long series of wars fought between Christians and Muslims over control of Palestine

Holy Land the European name for Palestine, the region where Jesus had lived

Pope Urban II head of the Roman Catholic Church who started the Crusades

King Richard I English king who led the third, ill-fated Crusade to seize Palestine

Saladin Turkish leader of the Muslim forces that prevented England from taking Palestine

Section Summary

CRUSADERS INVADE THE HOLY LAND

The **Crusades** were a long series of wars between Christians and Muslims in Southwest Asia. The Europeans fought the Muslims to retake Palestine. Christians call the region the **Holy Land** because it was where Jesus had lived, preached, and died.

> **Why did Christians call Palestine the "Holy Land?"**
> _____
> _____
> _____

For many years Palestine had been ruled by Muslims. In general, the Muslims did not bother Christians who visited the region. In the late 1000s, however, a new group of Turkish Muslims captured the city of Jerusalem. Pilgrims returning to Europe said that these Turks had attacked them.

Before long the Turks began to raid the Byzantine Empire. The Byzantine emperor asked **Pope Urban II** of the Roman Catholic Church for help. Although the Byzantines were Eastern Orthodox Christians and not Roman Catholic, the pope agreed to help.

> **Circle the name of the person who made the call to arms that led to the Crusades.**

Interactive Reader and Study Guide

Pope Urban called on Christians to retake the Holy Land from the Muslim Turks. Crusaders from all over Europe flocked to France to prepare to fight. Many peasants set out on the First Crusade. The Crusaders used the holy war as an excuse to kill many Jews along the way to Palestine. Some Christians at the time blamed the Jews for the death of Jesus. The peasant Crusaders were defeated by the professional Turk army. However, the nobles and knights were able to capture Palestine and set up four kingdoms there.

> Do you think the reason given for killing Jews was a mask for racial discrimination? Why or why not?
> _____
> _____
> _____
> _____

LATER CRUSADES FAIL

Within 50 years the Muslims had started taking land back from the Christians. The Europeans launched more Crusades, but these invasions ended in defeat and heavy losses for the Christians. The Third Crusade started as a group effort between the German, French, and English kings. But only **King Richard I** of England stayed on to fight. His opponent was the brilliant Turkish leader **Saladin**. Eventually, King Richard left Palestine, which was still under Muslim control. By 1291 Muslims had taken back Palestine. The Crusades were over.

> Circle the name of the European and Turkish leaders fighting in the Third Crusade.

CRUSADES CHANGE EUROPE

The Crusades increased trade between Europe and Asia. In some cases, the Crusades increased the power of the kings. But the main impact of the wars was divisive. The Crusades hurt the trust European Jews had developed with Christians. The Crusades also caused a major split between the Muslim and Christian worlds. Those tensions are still felt today.

> What do you think was the main impact the Crusades had on the world?
> _____
> _____
> _____
> _____

CHALLENGE ACTIVITY

Critical Thinking: Drawing Inferences Were the Crusades justified? Using what you now know about the impact the Crusades continue to have on our society today, write a brief position paper stating your opinion. Be sure to list facts and examples to support your point of view. **HSS Analysis Skills, CS 1, HI 2**

The Later Middle Ages

MAIN IDEAS

1. The Christian Church shaped society and politics in medieval Europe.
2. Orders of monks and friars did not like the church's political nature.
3. Church leaders helped build the first universities in Europe.
4. The church influenced the arts in medieval Europe.

 HSS 7.6

Students analyze the geographic, political, economic, religious, and social structures of the civilizations of Medieval Europe.

Key Terms and People

clergy church officials

religious order group of people who dedicate their lives to religion and follow common rules

Francis of Assisi founder of the Franciscan order

friars members of religious orders who lived and worked among the general public

Thomas Aquinas philosopher who showed how religious faith and reason could co-exist

natural law Thomas Aquinas's concept that God created a law that governed how the world operated

Section Summary

THE CHURCH SHAPES SOCIETY AND POLITICS

The **clergy** were very influential in medieval European culture and politics. For many people in the European Middle Ages, life revolved around the local church. Religious ceremonies like baptisms and weddings were key events in people's lives. Some people made pilgrimages, or journeys to religious locations.

The church owned a lot of land in Europe because many people left their property to the church when they died. In this way the church became a major feudal lord. Church officials often became political advisors to local rulers.

> List two key events in a person's life during the Middle Ages in which the local church was closely involved
>
> _____
> _____
> _____

Interactive Reader and Study Guide

MONKS AND FRIARS

Some people thought that the church was becoming too involved with politics. The monks of Cluny, France, established a new **religious order**. They dedicated their lives to religion with common rules. Other new orders followed. Women created their own religious communities in convents. Most monks lived apart from society, but two new religious orders developed for those who wanted to live and teach among people. These were the Dominicans, started by Dominic de Guzmán, and the Franciscans, started by **Francis of Assisi**. The members of these orders were called **friars**.

> Underline the sentence that explains why the monks of Cluny established a new religious order.

> How were the Dominicans and Franciscans different than the orders who lived in monasteries?
>
> _____
> _____
> _____
> _____

UNIVERSITIES ARE BUILT

Europe's first universities were built by the church. Religion, law, medicine, and philosophy were taught. Scholars wanted to establish a connection between religious faith and intellectual reason. The Dominican friar **Thomas Aquinas** wrote a reasoned argument for the existence of God. He also developed a philosophical system called **natural law** to show how God had ordered the world.

> Do you think it is necessary to be able to prove the existence of God? Why or why not?
>
> _____
> _____
> _____
> _____
> _____

THE CHURCH AND THE ARTS

The great Gothic cathedrals of late medieval Europe are among the most beautiful of all architectural achievements. Their spires and high ceilings and colorful stained glass windows are all designed to bring people closer to God. Everything inside the church, from the walls to the clergy's robes to the books used, were also works of art.

> Why do you think so much medieval European art was made for the church?
>
> _____
> _____
> _____
> _____

CHALLENGE ACTIVITY

Critical Thinking: Drawing Inferences Which medieval religious people do you agree with the most—those who became involved in politics, the monks who left society, or the friars who believed in working among the people? Write a one-page paper defending your views. **HSS Analysis Skills, HI 3, HI 5**

The Later Middle Ages

MAIN IDEAS

1. Magna Carta caused changes in England's government and legal system.

2. The Hundred Years' War led to political changes in England and France.

3. The Black Death, which swept through Europe in the Middle Ages, led to social changes.

 HSS 7.6
Students analyze the geographic, political, economic, religious, and social structures of the civilizations of Medieval Europe.

Key Terms and People

Magna Carta document written by English nobles and signed by King John listing rights the king could not ignore

Parliament lawmaking body that governs England

Hundred Years' War long-standing conflict between England and France during the 1300s and 1400s

Joan of Arc teenage peasant girl who rallied the French troops and turned the tide of the Hundred Years' War

Black Death deadly plague that killed millions of Europeans between 1347 and 1351

Section Summary

MAGNA CARTA CAUSES CHANGE IN ENGLAND

In 1215 a group of English nobles decided to force the king to respect their rights. They made King John approve a document listing rights the king could not ignore. This document was called the **Magna Carta**, or "Great Charter." Among these rights was that no one could be kept in jail without reason, and even the king must obey the law. This charter became a key principle of English government and an important step in the development of democracy.

The Magna Carta led to more changes. Faced with war and financial troubles, the kings turned to a council of nobles for advice and money. Before long, the council developed into **Parliament**, the lawmaking body that still governs England today.

Why do you think the agreement between King John and the nobles was called the "great charter?"

_____
_____
_____
_____

Who made up the original British Parliament?

_____
_____

Interactive Reader and Study Guide

Section 4, *continued*

THE HUNDRED YEARS' WAR

In Europe, kings were not giving up their power easily, but other events forced political change. A major event was the **Hundred Years' War**, a long conflict between England and France. The war started when the English king tried to take control of France's throne. England invaded France and won many key battles until a teenage peasant girl, **Joan of Arc**, rallied the French troops. The English caught and killed Joan, but the French eventually won the war. In England, the war helped increase the power of Parliament because the king needed Parliament's approval to raise money to pay for the war. In France, the king's power grew after the war.

> Why was Joan of Arc's feat truly remarkable? (List one of many possible reasons.)
> _____
> _____
> _____

THE BLACK DEATH

During the Hundred Years' War an even greater crisis arose. This crisis was the **Black Death**, a deadly plague that swept through Europe between 1347 and 1351. The plague originally came from central and eastern Asia. Traders unknowingly brought rats carrying the disease to Mediterranean ports. From there it quickly swept throughout much of Europe. Fleas that fed on infected rats passed on the plague to people.

Some historians think the Black Death killed a third of Europe's population—perhaps 25 million people. This caused sweeping changes all over Europe. The old manor system, already weakened by the growth of cities, collapsed. Plague survivors found their skills in demand and charged more for their labor. Instead of working for the rich, peasants now had other job opportunities.

> Underline the estimated number of victims of the Black Death.

> How did the Black Death ultimately benefit the survivors who lived on the manors?
> _____
> _____
> _____

CHALLENGE ACTIVITY

Critical Thinking: Drawing Inferences Many events during the later Middle Ages impacted the way we live today. Take one event discussed in this chapter and write a one-page paper explaining how our lives might be different if this event had *not* occurred. **HSS Analysis Skills, CS 1, HI 2, HI 3**

The Later Middle Ages

Section 5

MAIN IDEAS

1. The church reacted to challengers by punishing people who opposed its teachings.

2. Christians fought Moors in Spain and Portugal in an effort to drive all Muslims out of Europe.

3. Jews faced discrimination across Europe in the Middle Ages.

 HSS 7.6
Students analyze the geographic, political, economic, religious, and social structures of the civilizations of Medieval Europe.

Key Terms and People

heresy religious ideas that oppose accepted church teachings

Reconquista Christian efforts to retake Spain from the Muslim Moors

King Ferdinand Aragon prince who married Isabella of Castile to rule a united Spain

Queen Isabella Castilian princess who ruled Spain with her husband, Ferdinand of Aragon

Spanish Inquisition organization of priests charged with seeking out and punishing non-Christians

Section Summary

THE CHURCH REACTS TO CHALLENGERS

By around 1100, some Christians in Europe felt that the clergy were more concerned with money and land than with God. Others did not agree with the church's ideas. They began to preach their own ideas about religion.

Religious ideas that oppose church teachings are called **heresy**. Church officials sent priests and friars throughout Europe to find people who might be heretics. Most of these priests and friars tried to be fair, but some were not. Some tortured people until they confessed, even if they were innocent. Most people found guilty in these trials were fined or put in prison. Some, however, were put to death.

In the early 1200s, Pope Innocent III called for a crusade against heretics in southern France.

> Why do you think the church in late medieval Europe was so threatened by heresy?
>
> _____
> _____
> _____

> Do you think it was wise of the church authorities to leave the trials of heretics in the hands of individual priests and friars? Why or why not?
>
> _____
> _____
> _____

He encouraged the king and his knights to rid their country of heretics. The result was a bloody struggle that lasted about 20 years, destroying towns and cities and costing thousands of lives.

CHRISTIANS FIGHT THE MOORS

In Spain, the reign of the Muslim Moors collapsed in the 1000s. Christian kingdoms in Spain started a war to drive out the Muslims. They called their war **Reconquista** (reh-kahn-KEES-tuh), or reconquest. The kingdom of Castile was the first to free itself of Muslim rule. Portugal and Aragon soon followed. Castile and Aragon became united by the marriage of two royals, **King Ferdinand** of Aragon and **Queen Isabella** of Castile. Their union created the modern country of Spain. Portugal remained independent. In addition to banning Islam, Spain required all Jews to convert to Christianity or leave.

> What was the Reconquista?
> _____
> _____
> _____

Ferdinand and Isabella created the **Spanish Inquisition**, an organization of priests that looked for and punished non-Christians. The inquisition executed about 2,000 people in Spain and almost 1,400 more in Portugal.

> How many people in both Portugal and Spain died at the hands of the Spanish Inquisition?
> _____
> _____

JEWS FACE DISCRIMINATION

Spain's treatment of Jews spurred a more wide-scale attack on Jews. It had become common among many Christians to blame all Jews for the persecution and death of Jesus. Some people even blamed the Jews for the Black Death. In many kingdoms, Jews were driven out by angry mobs, and sometimes by the kings themselves. They had to flee from their homes or die.

> Name two things that some medieval Europeans blamed on the Jews.
> _____
> _____
> _____

CHALLENGE ACTIVITY

Critical Thinking: Drawing Inferences It is easy to see now that this period in history gave rise to intolerance and injustice for non-Christians. What could have led people to support such extreme and measures? Write a paper explaining how you think the church might have justified its methods. **HSS Analysis Skills, CR 5, HI 1, HI 5**

The Renaissance

HISTORY–SOCIAL SCIENCE STANDARDS

HSS 7.8 Students analyze the origins, accomplishments, and geographic diffusion of the Renaissance.

CHAPTER SUMMARY

Middle Ages	Renaissance
	Artists signed their work
Scholars and teachers were mostly clergy	Scholars and teachers were mostly laypeople
Books were handwritten	
The church taught that the earth was the center of universe	

COMPREHENSION AND CRITICAL THINKING

Use the answers to the following questions to fill in the graphic organizer above.

1. **Explain** Why did artists begin signing their work during the Renaissance?

   _____

   _____

2. **Identify Cause and Effect** What effect did the printing press have on the ability to study great works of literature?

   _____

   _____

3. **Evaluate** Why did education change so dramatically during the Renaissance?

   _____

   _____

4. **Draw a Conclusion** What big clash came between religion and science during the Renaissance?

   _____

   _____

The Renaissance

MAIN IDEAS

1. European trade with Asia increased in the 1300s.

2. Trade cities in Italy grew wealthy and competed against each other.

3. As Florence became a center for arts and learning, the Renaissance began.

 HSS 7.8
Students analyze the origins, accomplishments, and geographic diffusion of the Renaissance.

Key Terms and People

Marco Polo European explorer who traveled through Asia in the 1200s

Cosimo de' Medici wealthy banker who turned Florence into a center of arts, culture, and education

Renaissance period following the Middle Ages, characterized by renewed interest in Greek and Roman culture and an emphasis on secular rather than religious matters

Section Summary

TRADE WITH ASIA

It seems strange that the Black Death could have any positive results, but that is what happened. The disease did not damage farmland, buildings, ships, machines, or gold. People who survived could use these things to raise more food or make new products. Europe's economy began to grow again.

Prices went down and new products appeared in the markets. Some of these goods came from India, China, and other lands to the east. Traders brought many of these new goods across the Silk Road, an old caravan route from the Mediterranean Sea to China that had fallen into disuse. When the Mongols conquered China in the 1200s, they re-opened the Silk Road.

A traveler named **Marco Polo** spent 20 years in Asia and reignited an interest in the Far East. Marco Polo wrote a book on his travels, describing the many wonders of Asia, from coal to wonderful new spices. The book inspired many traders to seek those products themselves in Asia.

> Name one good result that came from the otherwise terrible Black Death.
> _____
> _____
> _____

> Why do you think the land route to China was called the Silk Road?
> _____
> _____
> _____
> _____

TRADE CITIES IN ITALY

By the 1300s four Italian cities had become major trading centers—Florence, Genoa, Milan, and Venice. Venice and Genoa were port cities. Huge ships brought spices and other luxuries from Asia into the cities' harbors.

> Circle the names of the Italian cities that were major ports for products from Asia.

These cities were also manufacturing centers. Different cities specialized in certain products. Venice produced glass. In Milan workers made weapons and silk. Florence was a center for weaving wool into cloth.

Italian cities were not unified under one ruler. Rich families, usually made wealthy by trade, controlled the government of each city.

> Who usually controlled the Italian cities during this time period?
> _____
> _____

FLORENCE

Florence developed a banking system that was used by merchants all over Europe. The richest of the bankers were the Medici family. By 1434 **Cosimo de´ Medici** (KOH-zee-moh day MED-I-chee) ruled Florence. Cosimo de´ Medici wanted Florence to be the most beautiful city in the world. He spent a great deal of money to make Florence a center of art, literature, and culture. In other cities, rich families tried to outdo the Medicis in support of the arts and learning.

This love of art and education was a key feature of the **Renaissance**, which means "rebirth." The Renaissance is the period following the Middle Ages. An interest in what the Greeks and Romans had learned and written was reborn. There was also a new emphasis on people as individuals.

> What historical period began when Cosimo de´ Medici beautified Florence?
> _____
> _____

CHALLENGE ACTIVITY

Critical Thinking: Drawing Inferences Why do you think beauty and education were so important to the Medici family of Florence? Write a short paper explaining your answer. **HSS Analysis Skills HI 1, HI 5**

Interactive Reader and Study Guide

The Renaissance

MAIN IDEAS

1. During the Italian Renaissance, people found new ways to see the world.
2. Italian writers contributed great works of literature.
3. Italian art and artists were among the finest in the world.
4. Science and education made advances during this time.

 HSS 7.8
Students analyze the origins, accomplishments, and geographic diffusion of the Renaissance.

Key Terms and People

humanism emphasis on human value and achievement

Dante Alighieri Italian poet who wrote *The Divine Comedy*

Niccolo Machiavelli political philosopher who wrote *The Prince*

perspective technique in art to represent a three-dimensional scene on a flat space so that it looks real

Michelangelo master artist who painted the ceiling of the Vatican's Sistine Chapel

Leonardo da Vinci master inventor, engineer, and artist who painted the Mona Lisa

Petrarch Renaissance poet and scholar who helped change education

Section Summary

NEW WAYS TO SEE THE WORLD

During the Middle Ages most people in Europe had devoted themselves to Christianity. In the Renaissance people began to see themselves and what they created as having value. This new emphasis on human value and achievement was called **humanism**. Renaissance humanists believed that people could do great things. This led to a revived interest in history and the writings of the ancient Greeks and Romans.

> How were humanists of the Renaissance different than the people of the Middle Ages?
> _____
> _____
> _____

ITALIAN WRITERS

Dante Alighieri (DAHN-tay ahl-eeg-YEH-ree) was an early Italian Renaissance writer. His major work, *The Divine Comedy,* tells of an imaginary journey

through the afterlife guided by the Greek poet
Virgil. *The Divine Comedy* was written in Italian,
the language spoken by the common people, rather
than Latin. A later writer, **Niccolo Machiavelli**
(neek-koh-LOH mahk-yah-VEL-lee), used his political
experience in his book *The Prince* to advise leaders
on how they should rule.

> In what language did Dante Alighieri write his book *The Divine Comedy?*
> _____
> _____

> Machiavelli was a politician. How do you think that experience helped him in writing *The Prince?*
> _____
> _____
> _____
> _____

ITALIAN ART AND ARTISTS

Renaissance artists painted and sculpted human
figures realistically. They developed the technique
of **perspective**, which shows a three-dimensional
scene on a flat surface so that it looks real. Two
artists from this time represent the ideal of the
Renaissance person, one who does everything well.
Michelangelo (mee-kay-LAHN-jay-loh) had many
talents—he designed buildings, wrote poetry,
carved sculptures, and painted magnificent pictures. **Leonardo da Vinci** was a true genius. He was
accomplished in painting, sculpture, architecture,
invention, engineering, and mapmaking.

> Underline the sentence that explains how perspective helped Renaissance artists draw more realistically.

SCIENCE AND EDUCATION

Renaissance scientific advances included the
important discovery that the earth revolves around
the sun. Education changed dramatically. During
the Renaissance, students learned the humanities,
including grammar, public speaking, poetry,
history, and the Greek and Latin languages. History
was one of the subjects that received more attention.
An early Renaissance poet and scholar named
Francesco Petrarca, usually called **Petrarch** (PE-
trahrk), was an early champion of studying history.

> How was education in the Renaissance different than education during the Middle Ages?
> _____
> _____
> _____
> _____

CHALLENGE ACTIVITY

Critical Thinking: Drawing Inferences Now is the time to stop and
think big—real big, like the Renaissance humanists did. Take a deep
breath and write for five minutes, listing every great thing you ever
might want to do in your life. List everything, however impossible. Keep
this list with you. **HSS Analysis Skills HI 1**

The Renaissance

MAIN IDEAS

1. Paper, printing, and new universities led to the spread of new ideas.
2. The ideas of the Northern Renaissance differed from those of the Italian Renaissance.
3. Literature beyond Italy also thrived in the Renaissance.

 HSS 7.8
Students analyze the origins, accomplishments, and geographic diffusion of the Renaissance.

Key Terms and People

Johann Gutenberg German inventor of the printing press with movable type

Christian humanism combination of humanism and Christianity

Desiderius Erasmus priest and Christian humanist who critiqued corrupt clergy

Albrecht Dürer German painter who is also known for his block printing

Miguel de Cervantes Spanish writer of *Don Quixote,* a novel that mocked medieval habits and customs

William Shakespeare English dramatist and poet inspired by the Renaissance

Section Summary

SPREAD OF NEW IDEAS

Individual travelers and artists helped spread the Renaissance from Italy throughout Europe. The development of printing was a major revolution. For the first time in history, thousands of people could read the same books and share ideas about them.

Papermaking came from China to the Middle East and from there to Europe. European factories were making paper by the 1300s. Because it was cheaper and easier to prepare, paper soon replaced the animal skins on which people had written before. Then in the mid-1400s a German named **Johann Gutenberg** (GOOT-uhn-berk) developed a printing press that used movable type. Each letter was a separate piece. A worker could fit letters into a frame, spread ink on the letters, and press a sheet of paper against the letters. An entire page was printed at once.

> **From where did the art of papermaking come?**
> _____
> _____

> **The Bible was the first book printed using Gutenberg's movable type. Why do you think that is so?**
> _____
> _____
> _____

Scholars from around the world attended Italy's universities. Teachers were humanists. Women did not study there, but they were encouraged to be educated in the classics at home.

THE NORTHERN RENAISSANCE

Scholars of northern Europe changed some Renaissance concepts. They often applied humanism to religious topics. They believed that human beings were valuable for their own sake, and that the church should treat people better. They called for church reform. This combination of humanism with religion is called **Christian humanism**. A Dutch priest, **Desiderius Erasmus** (des-I-DEER-ee-uhs i-RAZ-mus), published *The Praise of Folly,* criticizing corrupt clergy.

Northern artists also embraced realism. However, they had no access to Greek statues and their people looked normal, with physical flaws. German painter **Albrecht Dürer** (AWL-brekt DYUR-uhr) showed objects in great detail. He is also known for his prints, produced by carving designs onto a wooden block, then laying the image on ink and printing it many times.

> Why do you think Christian humanists called for church reform?
> _____
> _____
> _____
> _____

> Circle the name of a famous northern Renaissance painter who tried to make his work look realistic.

LITERATURE BEYOND ITALY

Like Dante, writers in other countries produced work in the native languages. In Spain **Miguel de Cervantes** wrote *Don Quixote*. In this book Cervantes poked fun at the romantic tales of the Middle Ages. The Renaissance also inspired the great English playwright and poet **William Shakespeare**.

> Why do you think Cervantes made fun of the ideas of the Middle Ages?
> _____
> _____
> _____
> _____

CHALLENGE ACTIVITY

Critical Thinking: Drawing Inferences How did the northerners build upon Renaissance ideas? Write a brief paragraph using specific examples from this section. **HSS Analysis Skills HI 1, HI 3**

The Reformation of Christianity

HISTORY–SOCIAL SCIENCE STANDARDS
HSS 7.9 Students analyze the historical developments of the Reformation.

CHAPTER SUMMARY

	led to	**the Protestant Reformation**
Protestant Reformation	led to	**the Lutheran Church and Calvinism**
Council of Trent	led to	**the Catholic Reformation**
Formation of the Jesuits	led to	

COMPREHENSION AND CRITICAL THINKING

Use the answers to the following questions to fill in the graphic organizer above.

1. Explain What was the general subject of Martin Luther's Ninety-Five Theses?

_____

_____

2. Identify Cause and Effect Why did the Lutherans break off from the Catholic Church and form their own church?

_____

_____

3. Evaluate How did the Catholic Church change as a result of the Protestant movement?

_____

_____

4. Draw a Conclusion What impacts of the Catholic Reformation can we still see in the world today?

_____

_____

The Reformation of Christianity

> **MAIN IDEAS**
>
> 1. The Catholic Church faced challengers who were upset with the behavior of Catholic clergy and with church practices.
>
> 2. Martin Luther urged reform in the Catholic Church, but he eventually broke away from the church.
>
> 3. Other reformers built on the ideas of early reformers to create their own churches.

 HSS 7.9
Students analyze the historical developments of the Reformation.

Key Terms and People

Reformation the reform movement against the Roman Catholic Church

indulgence a document sold by the church, excusing people from penalties for a sin they had committed

purgatory in Catholic theology, a place where souls went before going to heaven

Martin Luther priest who criticized the church abuses and started the Reformation

Protestants those who protested against the Catholic Church

John Calvin reformer who taught that common people should have a say in church policy

King Henry VIII English king who started the Church of England

Section Summary

THE CATHOLIC CHURCH FACES CHALLENGERS

By the late Renaissance some people began complaining about the Roman Catholic Church. This led to a movement called the **Reformation**.

During the Middle Ages the Roman Catholic Church had become one of the richest institutions in Europe, partly because it was exempt from paying taxes. Now many claimed that the church had grown too rich. Some criticized priests for not even knowing basic church teachings. Others felt that church officials were too involved in politics and neglected religious duties.

The sale of **indulgences** was a serious problem. The church claimed the indulgence did not forgive a

> "Reformation" is a noun. What verb does it build on?
>
> _____
>
> _____

> Why were some people horrified by the church practice of selling indulgences?
>
> _____
>
> _____
>
> _____

person for sins, but reduced the punishment that a person would receive for sins in **purgatory**.

MARTIN LUTHER URGES REFORM

In 1517 a priest named **Martin Luther** nailed a list of 95 complaints about the church to the door of a church in Wittenberg, Germany. The document criticized many church practices, especially the sale of indulgences. Luther's complaints angered Pope Leo X, who branded Luther a heretic and excommunicated him.

> Underline the sentence that tells how the pope responded to Luther's protest.

Luther's ideas eventually led to a split in the Catholic Church. Luther thought that anyone could have a direct relationship with God. He called for a priesthood of all believers. Those who sided with Luther and protested against the church became known as **Protestants**. Some of those who followed Luther's teachings founded their own church and became known as the Lutherans. Luther's ideas appealed to some nobles. The support of these nobles soon made Lutheranism the dominant church in northern Germany.

> Define "Protestant."
> _____
> _____
> _____
> _____

OTHER REFORMERS

William Tyndale, an English professor, thought that everyone should be able to read the Bible. Tyndale's translation of the Bible into English led to his execution. **John Calvin** taught predestination, the idea that God knew who would be saved even before they were born. **King Henry VIII** of England started a new church, the Church of England, because the pope would not allow him to divorce and remarry.

> Why did King Henry VIII start a new church?
> _____
> _____

CHALLENGE ACTIVITY

Critical Thinking: Drawing Inferences Imagine how you might feel if you were Martin Luther, pinning his complaints to the church door. Think of something you care strongly about and write a list of things that you would like to change. Your list does not have to contain 95 items, but it should have at least 10. **HSS Analysis Skills CR 2, CR 4**

The Reformation of Christianity

Section 2

MAIN IDEAS

1. The influence of the church created a Catholic culture in Spain.
2. Catholic reforms emerged in response to the Reformation.
3. Missionaries worked to spread Catholic teachings.

 HSS 7.9
Students analyze the historical developments of the Reformation.

Key Terms and People

Catholic Reformation the effort to reform the Catholic Church from within

Ignatius of Loyola former soldier who founded the Jesuit order

Jesuits religious order founded to serve the pope and spread Catholic teachings

Francis Xavier Jesuit missionary who went to Asia and brought Catholicism to parts of India and Japan

Section Summary

CATHOLIC CULTURE IN SPAIN

The effort to reform the Roman Catholic Church from within is called the **Catholic Reformation**. Throughout the late-1500s and the 1600s, Catholic leaders worked to strengthen the church and combat the spread of Protestantism. Many leaders came from southern Europe, especially Spain.

For centuries the region we now call Spain had been home to three religions. Christians, Muslims, and Jews had all lived and worked together there, making great advances in art, literature, philosophy, mathematics, and science. But in 1492 the new king and queen of Spain unified the country. The new Spanish government forced all Jews and Muslims to convert to Catholicism or leave Spain. The dreaded Spanish Inquisitors hunted down and punished any non-Catholics who remained in Spain. The Spanish clergy were the first to fight against the Protestant Reformation.

> Underline the name for efforts to reform the Catholic Church from within.

> Why do you think the Catholic Reformation happen first in Spain?
> _____
> _____
> _____

Interactive Reader and Study Guide

CATHOLIC REFORMS

In an attempt to win back support for the church, Catholic reformers created many new religious orders in southern Europe in the 1500s. **Ignatius** (ig-NAY-shuhs) **of Loyola** founded the Society of Jesus, or the **Jesuits**. Ignatius had been a soldier and he expected his Jesuits to be as disciplined as soldiers in their religious duties.

> **What in the life of Ignatius led him to require great discipline of his Jesuits?**
> _____
> _____

Catholic leaders assembled at the Council of Trent to discuss reforms in the church. This council met three times between 1545 and 1563. Bishops were now required to live in the areas they oversaw. The Council of Trent rejected Luther, Calvin, and other Protestant reformers. The pope also created special religious courts designed to try any Protestants for heresy, and threatened excommunication for those who read Protestant books.

MISSIONARIES SPREAD CATHOLIC TEACHINGS

Rather than change the church, many Catholics decided to dedicate their lives to helping it grow by becoming missionaries. Many missionaries were Jesuits, including the most important, the priest **Francis Xavier**. He traveled throughout Asia in the mid-1500s, bringing Catholicism to parts of India and Japan. As a result of his efforts, many people in those regions became Catholics. Catholic missionaries baptized millions of people around the world. Through their efforts the effects of the Catholic Reformation reached far beyond Europe.

> **Where did Francis Xavier go to convert Catholics?**
> _____
> _____

CHALLENGE ACTIVITY

Critical Thinking: Drawing Inferences Do you think the Catholics did a good job of reforming the church from within? Is it possible to reform an institution from within? Write a paper about either the Catholic Reformation or any other internal reformation of an institution that you know, citing whether or not the reforms were effective and why.
HSS Analysis Skills CR 1, CR 3, HI 1

The Reformation of Christianity

Section 3

MAIN IDEAS

1. Religious division occurred within Europe and the Americas.

2. Religious wars broke out between Protestants and Catholics.

3. Social changes were a result of the Reformation.

 HSS 7.9
Students analyze the historical developments of the Reformation.

Key Terms and People

Huguenots French Protestants

Edict of Nantes law granting religious freedom in most of France

Thirty Years' War long series of wars between Catholics and Protestants involving much of Europe

congregation church assembly

federalism sharing of power between national and local governments

Section Summary

RELIGIOUS DIVISION

At the beginning of the 1500s nearly all of Europe was Catholic. But the situation had changed dramatically 100 years later. Most of northern Europe had become Protestant.

In many southern European countries nearly everyone remained Catholic. In the north, countries such as England, Scotland, and the Scandinavian countries, most people were Protestant. However, the emperor of the Holy Roman Empire allowed each prince to choose the religion of his territory. As a result, the empire became a patchwork of small kingdoms, some Catholic and some Protestant. Keeping peace between kingdoms with different religions was often a difficult task.

> Which part of Europe became predominantly Protestant in the span of merely 100 years?
> _____
> _____

> Regarding religious freedom, how did the Holy Roman Empire differ from Spain?
> _____
> _____
> _____

RELIGIOUS WARS

Disagreements about religion and violence often went hand in hand. In France, although most

Section 3, *continued*

people remained Catholic, some became Protestants. These French Protestants were called **Huguenots** (HYOO-guh-nahts). The king of France outlawed the Huguenots.

A series of conflicts between Catholics and Huguenots led to years of bloody war. The worst incident was the St. Bartholomew's Day Massacre in 1572. In one night, Catholic rioters killed about 3,000 Protestants in Paris. In the days that followed, riots broke out all over France and thousands more Protestants were killed. The war between Catholics and Protestants in France ended in 1598 with the **Edict of Nantes**, which granted religious freedom to most of France.

The Holy Roman Empire fared no better. Starting in Prague with Protestants overthrowing their Catholic leader, the revolt evolved into the **Thirty Years' War**, a long series of wars that involved many European countries.

> Why do you think the Huguenots chose to fight?
> _____
> _____
> _____

> Where did the Thirty Years' War start?
> _____
> _____

SOCIAL CHANGES

Before the Reformation, most Europeans had no voice in governing the Catholic Church. But most Protestant churches did not have priests, bishops, or other clergy. Instead, each **congregation**, or church assembly, made its own rules. Now for the first time people began to think that their own ideas were important. This led to demands for more political power, in the form of **federalism**, the sharing of power between national and local governments. People became more willing to question authority and figure out things on their own.

> Underline the sentence that explains how religious reform led to political reform.

CHALLENGE ACTIVITY

Critical Thinking: Drawing Inferences You have been reading a lot about the Reformation period, both from within and without. What is the most important thing that has come out of the Reformation that still impacts society today? Write a one-page essay explaining your answer. **HSS Analysis Skills CS 1, HR 1, HI 1**

The Scientific Revolution

HISTORY–SOCIAL SCIENCE STANDARDS
HSS 7.10 Students analyze the historical developments of the Scientific Revolution and its lasting effect on religious, political, and cultural institutions.

CHAPTER SUMMARY

THE SCIENTIFIC REVOLUTION

1492—Columbus discovers North America, causes people to question teachings of the ancient Greeks

1590—Zacharias Janssen invents the microscope

1609—Galileo uses the telescope to study planets

1687—Newton publishes *Principia Mathematica*

1543—Corpernicus publishes his theory of a sun-centered solar system, disputes Ptolemy's long-held theory that the earth is the center of the universe

1605–1644—Writings by Francis Bacon and René Descartes provide the basis of the "scientific method"

1616—Galileo put on trial for his scientific theories

COMPREHENSION AND CRITICAL THINKING

Use information from the graphic organizer to answer the following questions.

1. Explain Who was the first scientist to refute the theories of the ancient Greek scholar Ptolemy?

_____

_____

2. Identify Cause and Effect Why did Christopher Columbus's discovery of the new world cause doubt among scholars about ancient Greek authorities?

_____

_____

3. Evaluate Why do you think the Catholic Church was threatened by the new science?

_____

_____

4. Draw a Conclusion How did the Scientific Revolution impact non-scientific disciplines?

_____

_____

_____

The Scientific Revolution

Section 1

MAIN IDEAS

1. The Scientific Revolution marked the birth of modern science.

2. The roots of the Scientific Revolution can be traced to ancient Greece, the Muslim world, and Europe.

 HSS 7.10

Students analyze the historical developments of the Scientific Revolution and its lasting effects on religious, political, and cultural institutions.

Key Terms and People

Scientific Revolution series of events that led to the birth of modern science

science a particular way of gaining knowledge about the world

theories explanations developed by scientists to explain observable facts

Ptolemy Greek astronomer whose work was based on observation and logic

rationalists people who looked at the world in a rational, reasonable, and logical way

alchemy a forerunner of chemistry

Academic Vocabulary

logical reasoned, well thought out

Section Summary

THE BIRTH OF MODERN SCIENCE

During the 1500s and 1600s, a handful of brilliant individuals built the foundations of science as we know it today. Some historians consider the development of science the single most important event in the intellectual history of humankind. The series of events that led to the birth of modern science is called the **Scientific Revolution**. It was a radical idea. It was a completely different way of looking at the world.

Before the Scientific Revolution, most educated people relied on the teachings of the ancient Greek and Catholic Church authorities. Afterward, people began to gain knowledge by observing the world around them and forming logical conclusions.

The word **science** is Latin for "knowledge." Science is a particular way of gaining knowledge

> **What was so revolutionary about the Scientific Revolution?**
>
> _____
> _____
> _____
> _____

about the world. Scientists identify facts about the
world by observation and then develop **theories**,
which are explanations based on the facts. Theories
must be tested to see if they are true. Before the
Scientific Revolution, this way of learning about the
world did not exist.

> Underline the two sentences that explain the basic method of science.

ROOTS OF THE REVOLUTION

The concept of science found its roots in ideas
from the past. The Greek philosopher Aristotle,
who wrote about geography and astronomy, made
a great contribution to future science when he
stressed that people should observe the world
carefully and make careful, logical conclusions.

> Underline the phrase that declares what method Aristotle recommended to explain the world.

The ancient Greek astronomer **Ptolemy** put these
ideas into practice. He studied the skies and offered
theories to explain what he saw. As a geographer,
he made the most accurate maps of his time based
on real world observations. Thinkers like these are
called **rationalists**, people who look at the world in
a rational, reasonable, or **logical** way.

European scholars were able to study the ancient
Greek writings because Muslim scholars had already
translated the writings and added their own ideas.
Early religious scholars also wrote about the classics.
The Jewish scholar Maimonides (my-MAHN-uh-
deez) and the Christian scholar Thomas Aquinas
tried to apply Greek philosophy and theories to
their religions. The humanists spent much time
observing the natural world. There was also a
growing interest in **alchemy** (AL-kuh-mee), an early
forerunner of chemistry. All this information was
borrowed by science later.

> Name two scholars who thought and wrote about the Greek and Roman classics in relation to religion.
>
> _____
>
> _____
>
> _____

CHALLENGE ACTIVITY

Critical Thinking: Drawing Inferences Write a one-page paper
describing a world without any rationalist ideas. How would people
think, feel, and react? What options would they have for understanding
the world around them? **HSS Analysis Skills CS 1, HI 1**

The Scientific Revolution

Section 2

MAIN IDEAS

1. The discovery of the Americas led scholars to doubt ancient Greek ideas.
2. Advances in astronomy were key events in the Scientific Revolution.
3. Sir Isaac Newton developed laws that explained much of the natural world.
4. New inventions helped scientists study the natural world.

 HSS 7.10
Students analyze the historical developments of the Scientific Revolution and its lasting effects on religious, political, and cultural institutions.

Key Terms and People

Nicolaus Copernicus Polish astronomer who learned that the earth and planets orbited the sun, contradicting the theories of Greek astronomer Ptolemy

Tycho Brahe Danish astronomer who made detailed charts of the stars' movements

Johannes Kepler German astronomer who proved and elaborated upon Copernicus's theory about the movements of the planets

Galileo Galilei Italian scientist and astronomer who subjected his theories to rigorous experiments

Sir Isaac Newton English scientist who discovered that physical laws, like the law of gravity, govern the natural world

barometer scientific instrument that measures air pressure

Section Summary

DISCOVERY LEADS TO DOUBT

During the Renaissance, scholars studied the ancient Greek and Roman authorities. No one thought to question their information until 1492, when Christopher Columbus, a sailor and explorer, came upon something the ancients never imagined existed—another continent. Scholars began to question the ancient authorities for the first time.

> Why do you think Columbus's discovery of the new world cast doubt on the writings of ancient authorities?
>
> _____
> _____
> _____
> _____

ADVANCES IN ASTRONOMY

In 1543 Polish astronomer **Nicolaus Copernicus** published *On the Revolution of the Celestial Spheres,* the first book to contradict the respected Greek astronomer Ptolemy. According to Ptolemy, the

> Which Greek Astronomer did Copernicus prove wrong? (Circle the name.)

Interactive Reader and Study Guide

earth was the center of the universe. But Copernicus studied the planets and saw that this was unlikely. He asked himself whether the planets might orbit around the sun. This theory fit his observations.

Astronomer **Tycho Brahe** made detailed notes of the positions of the stars. **Johannes Kepler** both supported and corrected the work of Copernicus. His studies proved that the planets did orbit the sun. But Kepler also learned that the planets move in elliptical, not circular, orbits.

Galileo Galilei was one of the most important scientists of the Scientific Revolution. He was the first person to study the planets with a telescope. He also rigorously tested his theories with experiments.

> Why do you think the celestial observations of Tycho Brahe were important?
>
> _____
> _____
> _____
> _____

SIR ISAAC NEWTON

With his book *Principia Mathematica,* published in 1687, **Sir Isaac Newton** distinguished himself as perhaps the most important scientist of all time. He reviewed and evaluated all previous scientific work, coupled it with his own observations, and developed four theories about how the natural world worked. These theories have been proven so many times, they have become laws, like the law of gravity. He also developed mathematical calculus.

> Name one of Sir Isaac Newton's theories that has been tested so many times it is recognized as a scientific law.
>
> _____
> _____

NEW INVENTIONS

New inventions aided in the observations of scientists. The microscope, the telescope, and the **barometer** helped scientists observe their surroundings more accurately.

> Why do you think such inventions as the microscope, the telescope, and the barometer improved scientific theory?
>
> _____
> _____
> _____
> _____

CHALLENGE ACTIVITY

Critical Thinking: Drawing Inferences Conduct your own experiments with gravity. Drop several objects—like a pencil, an apple, and a book—from different heights. Make observations about each object as it falls.
HSS Analysis Skills CR 2, HI 5

The Scientific Revolution

Section 3

MAIN IDEAS

1. The ideas of Francis Bacon and René Descartes led to clarify the scientific method.
2. Science influenced new ideas about government.
3. Science and religion developed a sometimes uneasy relationship.

 HSS 7.10
Students analyze the historical developments of the Scientific Revolution and its lasting effects on religious, political, and cultural institutions.

Key Terms and People

Francis Bacon English philosopher who proposed that science should be pursued in a systematic fashion

René Descartes French philosopher who said nothing should be accepted if not proven true

scientific method step-by-step procedure for performing experiments or research

hypothesis a proposed solution to a problem that must be tested

Academic Vocabulary

procedure a series of steps taken to accomplish a task
principles basic beliefs, rules, or laws

Section Summary

BACON, DESCARTES AND THE SCIENTIFIC METHOD

Science has become the most established and reliable way of learning about the natural world. The acceptance of this fact of modern life is due to the work of **Francis Bacon** and **René Descartes**.

Bacon was an English philosopher and politician who recognized how much new knowledge could be gained from the systematic use of science. He tried to persuade the king of England to fund scientific research. Descartes, a French philosopher, argued that nothing should be accepted it if were not proven true. Observation and theory are not enough, he said, because people could be tricked by

Underline the sentence that states a political move made by Francis Bacon to advance science.

What was Descartes' basic theory about knowledge?

_____

_____

_____

their senses. People must use clear thinking and reason to establish proof.

Scientists today employ the **scientific method**, a clear, step-by-step **procedure** for performing experiments and scientific research. This involves gathering information then forming and testing a **hypothesis** before coming to a conclusion.

> Why is testing a hypothesis an important part of the scientific method?
> _____
> _____
> _____

SCIENCE AND GOVERNMENT

Science had a profound impact on many non-scientific subjects. Philosophers recognized that human reason, or logic, was a powerful tool that could be applied to solve human problems. One way of solving these problems was by changing government. This marked the beginning of democratic thought. If laws govern the natural world, people surmised, maybe laws also govern human behavior. Determining those laws could help solve problems like war and poverty. What more equalizing **principle** exists than the idea that all humans were subject to the same laws?

> Why did applying the scientific model to human behavior lead to the idea people are equal?
> _____
> _____
> _____

SCIENCE AND RELIGION

The powerful Catholic Church regarded some of the advances of science with suspicion. Many of the new ideas contradicted the church's teachings and undermined and weakened its authority. The best-known church-science conflict was the case of Galileo, who was tried and threatened with torture unless he agreed with the church that the earth was the center of the universe and did not move. Ironically, Galileo and other scientists did not think science went against religion. They believed it helped people understand God's creation.

> As Galileo left the church courtroom where he was tried for his theories, he was heard to mutter, "Yet it does move." To what was he referring?
> _____
> _____

CHALLENGE ACTIVITY

Critical Thinking: Drawing Inferences Do you think human behavior is governed by natural laws? Write an essay describing why you do or do not believe this hypothesis. Remember to test your opinion before making conclusions. **HSS Analysis Skills CR 2, CR 3, CR 4**

The Early Americas

HISTORY–SOCIAL SCIENCE STANDARDS
HSS 7.7 Students compare and contrast the geographic, political, economic, religious, and social structures of the Meso-American and Andean civilizations.
HSS Analysis Skill HR3 Distinguish relevant from irrelevant, essential from incidental, and verifiable from unverifiable information.

CHAPTER SUMMARY

The domestication of maize	led to	**settled life in Mesoamerica**
The rise of villages and towns	led to	**the development of a trading network**
The growth of cities	led to	**new discoveries in science, math, and writing**
Warfare and drought	led to	**the collapse of the Maya civilization**

COMPREHENSION AND CRITICAL THINKING

Use information from the graphic organizer to answer the following questions.

1. Explain What and where was the first domesticated crop grown in the Americas?

_____

2. Identify Cause and Effect How did the development of corn change the lives of the early Americans?

_____

3. Evaluate How did the Maya show their respect for corn?

_____

_____

4. Draw a Conclusion How did the growth cycle of corn influence our modern concept of a 365-day year?

_____

_____

_____

The Early Americas

Section 1

MAIN IDEAS

1. The geography of the Americas is varied with a wide range of landforms.

2. The first people to arrive in the Americas were hunter-gatherers.

2. The development of farming led to early settlement in the Americas.

 HSS 7.7
Students compare and contrast the geographic, political, economic, religious, and social structures of the Meso-American and Andean civilizations.

Key Terms and People

Mesoamerica region that includes the southern part of what is now Mexico and parts of the northern countries of Central America

maize corn

Section Summary

GEOGRAPHY OF THE AMERICAS

The Americas are made up of two continents, North America and South America. These continents have a wide range of landforms. The first people of the Americas were hunter-gatherers. They depended on the geography of the land to find food.

Historians call the cultural region in the southern part of North America **Mesoamerica**. Mesoamerica extended from the middle of modern-day Mexico south to Central America. The region's many rain forests and rivers created fertile farmland. The first farmers in the Americas domesticated plants there.

> Underline the description of the land included in the area called Mesoamerica.

THE FIRST PEOPLE ARRIVE

No one is sure how people first arrived in the Americas. Some scientists believe they came from Asia some time before 12,000 BC, walking over a land bridge that crossed the Bering Strait. Other historians think the first Americans arrived by sea.

The earliest people were hunter-gatherers. These people survived on wild buffalo and other animals,

> Fill in the blanks: Some scientists believe the first Americans arrived by
>
> _____
>
> while others believe they arrived by
>
> _____
>
> _____

Section 1, *continued*

as well as fruits, nuts, and wild grains. They moved frequently, depending upon where food was most plentiful. Some people eventually settled along the coastal areas, fishing and planting different types of seeds to see which would grow best. This changed early American life.

> Circle the main factor that changed life in the early Americas.

FARMING AND SETTLEMENT

The experiments with seeds led to farming. This allowed people to live in one place permanently. The first farming settlements were in Mesoamerica. By 3500 BC Mesoamericans were growing **maize**, or corn. Later they learned to grow squash and beans. As in other areas of the world, once people settled, towns and cities were created. The population grew and societies began to develop religion, art, and trade opportunities.

> Why does experimenting with seeds lead to farming?
> _____
> _____
> _____
> _____

Historians believe that the Olmec (OHL-mek) were the first Mesoamericans to live in villages. Some Olmec lived in bigger towns, which were the centers of government and religion. They built pyramids and huge stone sculptures of their rulers and gods. They developed a large trading network.

Archaeological evidence suggests the Olmec may have created the first written language in the Americas and designed a calendar. Later civilizations that traded with the Olmec were influenced by Olmec culture. Other civilizations developed in South America around farming. The methods for growing maize spread throughout South and North America.

> What Olmec achievement had the most lasting effect on American civilizations?
> _____
> _____

CHALLENGE ACTIVITY

Critical Thinking: Drawing Inferences Draw a timeline showing how the first human civilization developed in the Americas. Start with the two theories of how humans first arrived to the Americas, and end with the establishment of the Olmec civilization. **HSS Analysis Skills HR 3, HR 5, HI 4**

The Early Americas

Section 2

MAIN IDEAS

1. Geography affected early Maya civilization.

2. The Maya Classic Age was characterized by great cities, trade, and warfare.

3. Maya civilization declined, and historians have several theories as to why.

 HSS 7.7
Students compare and contrast the geographic, political, economic, religious, and social structures of the Meso-American and Andean civilizations.

Key Terms and People

obsidian a sharp, glasslike volcanic rock found in Mesoamerica

Pacal Maya king who dedicated a temple to record his achievements as ruler

Section Summary

GEOGRAPHY AFFECTS EARLY MAYA

The Maya (MY-uh) civilization developed in the lowlands of Mesoamerica around 1000 BC. Thick forests covered the area, so the Maya had to cut down trees to farm. The forest was also a source of many resources, including animals for food and wood for building materials.

The Maya lived in villages. The Maya began trading such items as woven cloth and **obsidian**, a sharp, glasslike volcanic rock. By AD 200 the Maya were building the first large cities in the Americas.

> Circle the approximate date that Maya civilization developed in the Mesoamerican lowlands.

MAYA CLASSIC AGE

Maya civilization reached its height between AD 250 and 900, a period called the Classic Age. During this time there were more than more than 40 Maya cities. Each city had populations of 5,000 to 50,000 people. The Maya traded for things that could not be found in their own part of Mesoamerica. The lowlands had many crops and wood products. The highlands had valuable stones like jade and obsidian.

The Maya built large stone pyramids, temples, and palaces. Some of these buildings honored

> List three valued Maya exports.
> _____
> _____
> _____
> _____

Interactive Reader and Study Guide

Name _____ Class _____ Date _____

Section 2, *continued*

local kings. A temple built in the city of Palenque (pah-LENG-kay) honored the king **Pacal** (puh-KAHL). Artists decorated the temple with paintings and carvings celebrating his achievements as ruler. The Maya built canals to bring water to the cities. They shaped hillsides into flat terraces so they could grow crops on them. The Maya also paved the cities' central plazas. Most cities had a ball court to watch a game the Maya had learned from the Olmec.

The Maya did not have a central government. Kings governed each city separately. Cities often fought each other over territory and resources. This warfare was violent and destructive. Some historians believe warfare led to the end of the Maya civilization.

> How do historians know about the rule of the Maya king Pacal?
> _____
> _____
> _____
> _____

> Do you think a central government might have saved Maya civilization? Why or why not?
> _____
> _____
> _____
> _____

MAYA CIVILIZATION DECLINES

Maya civilization began to collapse in the 900s. They stopped building large buildings and left the cities for the countryside. Historians are not sure why this happened, but there are several theories.

Some historians believe that Maya farmers kept planting the same crop over and over, which weakened the soil and caused drought. This may have caused more competition and war between the cities. Others think that the Maya kings made their people build huge temples or farm for them. The people got tired of working for the kings, so they rebelled. There were probably many factors that led to the decline of the Maya civilization.

> List two factors that may have contributed to the decline of the Maya civilization.
> _____
> _____
> _____

CHALLENGE ACTIVITY

Critical Thinking: Drawing Inferences One of the sources of information that historians have about the Maya comes from Maya kings like Pacal, who dedicated an entire temple to his achievements. If you were to dedicate a building to honor your life, what would it look like? Draw a picture of a building, including paintings and carvings that might be included on the walls. Think about what would be helpful to historians in the future who might want to reconstruct early 21st century life. **HSS Analysis Skills CS 3, CR 3, HI 5**

Interactive Reader and Study Guide

The Early Americas

Section 3

MAIN IDEAS

1. Roles in Maya society were based on a complex class structure.
2. Religion in Maya society was often bloody.
3. The Maya made achievements in art, science, math, and writing.

 HSS 7.7
Students compare and contrast the geographic, political, economic, religious, and social structures of the Meso-American and Andean civilizations.

Key Terms and People

observatories buildings designed to study astronomy and view the stars

Popol Vuh a book containing legends and some history of the Maya civilization

Section Summary

ROLES IN MAYA SOCIETY

The Maya had a complex social structure. The upper and lower classes led very different lives. Kings held the highest position. Priests, warriors, and merchants made up the upper class.

The Maya believed that their rulers were related to the gods. Men and women could be rulers, but they had to have been born into a royal family. Priests were also born into their roles. Priests were highly educated. They used their knowledge of astronomy and mathematics to plan religious ceremonies. The warriors fought the battles and the merchants directed trade. Together, these four groups controlled political, economic, and religious life for the Maya.

Most Maya belonged to lower-class farming families. They lived in little houses outside the cities. Girls were taught to run the household. Men hunted and farmed. Maya farmers were required to serve the upper class. They had to give up some of their crops and make goods for the upper class. They were also used as labor to build temples. Slaves held the lowest position in Maya society.

> Underline the names of the groups who made up the upper classes of Maya society.

> List four ways in which Maya farmers served the upper class.
> _____
> _____
> _____
> _____
> _____

Interactive Reader and Study Guide

RELIGION

The Maya worshipped many gods. They believed that each god represented a different area of life. The Maya believed that their kings spoke with the gods.

The Maya believed the gods could either help them or hurt them, so they tried to keep the gods happy. They thought that the gods needed blood, so everyone gave blood by piercing their skin or tongue. Special rituals of blood giving were held at births, weddings, and funerals. On special occasions the Maya believed the gods needed extra amounts of blood. They made human sacrifices to the gods.

> What did the Maya think their gods wanted in order to be appeased?
> _____
> _____

ACHIEVEMENTS

Maya achievements in art, architecture, math, science, and writing were remarkable. They did not have metal tools or wheeled vehicles, but they built huge stone structures. They are known for their stone carvings and jade and gold jewelry.

More important, though, are the advances the Maya made in astronomy and the development of the modern calendar. They built **observatories** for their priests to study the stars. They learned that the year had about 365 days. They developed a number system to go along with their calendar and record important events in their history.

> What did the Maya use their special numbering system for?
> _____
> _____
> _____

The Maya also developed a writing system similar to Egyptian hieroglyphics. They wrote on bark paper and carved records onto stone tablets. After the Spanish arrived, the legends and history of the Maya were written in a book called the **Popol Vuh** (poh-pohl VOO).

> Underline the phrase that describes the contents of the Popol Vuh.

CHALLENGE ACTIVITY

Critical Thinking: Drawing Inferences You are a Maya astronomer. List the twelve months of the year. Then under each month, write three astronomical events that might indicate a repeated cycle.
HSS Analysis Skills CS 3, HI 6

The Aztec and Inca Empires

HISTORY–SOCIAL SCIENCE STANDARDS

HSS 7.7 Students compare and contrast the geographic, political, economic, religious, and social structures of the Meso-American and Andean civilizations.

CHAPTER SUMMARY

Comparing Inca and Aztec Cultures

Inca

taxes paid in labor

no written language

_____

Aztec

built a large empire

_____

_____

taxes paid in gold, silver, or food

_____

economy based on trade

COMPREHENSION AND CRITICAL THINKING

Use the answers to the following questions to fill in the graphic organizer above.

1. Explain Name at least three differences and three similarities between the Aztec and Inca civilizations.

_____

2. Identify Cause and Effect How did the Aztecs build their empire?

_____

3. Draw a Conclusion Both the Inca and Aztec empires were destroyed by Spanish conquistadors. Although they were greatly outnumbered, how were the conquistadors able to conquer these mighty empires?

_____

_____

Interactive Reader and Study Guide

The Aztec and Inca Empires

Section 1

MAIN IDEAS
1. The Aztecs built an empire through warfare and trade, and created an impressive capital city in Mesoamerica.
2. Hernán Cortés conquered the Aztec Empire.

 HSS 7.7
Students compare and contrast the geographic, political, economic, religious, and social structures of the Meso-American and Andean civilizations.

Key Terms and People

causeways raised paths across water or wet ground

conquistadors Spanish soldiers and explorers

Hernán Cortés Spanish conquistador leader who conquered the Aztec Empire

Moctezuma II Aztec ruler who mistook Cortés for a god, leading to the Aztec's downfall

Section Summary

THE AZTECS BUILD AN EMPIRE

The first Aztecs were poor farmers from northern Mexico. They migrated south in the 1100s. Other tribes had taken the farmland, so the Aztecs settled on a swampy island in the middle of Lake Texcoco (tays-KOH-koh). By the early 1500s, the Aztecs ruled the most powerful empire in Mesoamerica.

War was key to the Aztecs' rise to power. The fierce Aztec warriors conquered many towns. The Aztecs made the people in the cities they conquered pay tribute with goods like cotton, gold, or food. This system was the basis of the Aztec economy. The Aztecs also controlled a huge trade network. Most towns in the empire had a market.

Nowhere was the Aztec Empire's power and wealth more visible than in its capital, Tenochtitlán (tay-NAWCH-teet-LAHN). The city's island location made travel and trade difficult, so the Aztecs built three wide **causeways** connecting the island to the shore. The water around the capital

> Where were the humble origins of the mighty Aztecs?
>
> _____
>
> _____

> What were the two key ways that the Aztecs became rich, even if they did not have their own farmland?
>
> _____
>
> _____

Interactive Reader and Study Guide

was undrinkable. For fresh water, the Aztecs built
a stone channel to bring water from far away. With
little farmland available, they built "floating gardens"
on rafts tied to trees in the water.

> Underline the colorful phrase that describes the ingenious farming method developed by the Aztecs.

At its height, Tenochtitlán was one of the world's
largest cities, with some 200,000 people. The city
featured a stunning array of temples and palaces,
and a busy market. But the arrival of Europeans
soon destroyed the city—and the Aztec Empire.

CORTÉS CONQUERS THE AZTECS

In the late 1400s Spanish explorers and soldiers
called **conquistadors** arrived in the Americas,
seeking gold and desiring to spread their religion.
Hernán Cortés (er-NAHN kawr-TAYS) led
conquistadors into Mexico in 1519. The ruler of
the Aztecs, **Moctezuma II** (MAWK-tay-SOO-mah),
thought Cortés was a god. Moctezuma sent Cortés
many gifts, including gold. Wanting more gold,
Cortés marched to the Aztec capital. When he got
there Moctezuma welcomed him, but Cortés took
the emperor prisoner.

> Why do you think Aztec leader Moctezuma II invited Hernán Cortés into the capital city?
> _____
> _____
> _____

> How did Cortés' respond to Moctezuma's invitation?
> _____
> _____
> _____

Enraged, the Aztecs attacked the Spanish and
drove them out of the city. In the confusion
Moctezuma was killed. Before long Cortés and his
men came back, this time with reinforcements. In
1521 they conquered Tenochtitlán.

To defeat the empire, the Spanish allied with
tribes who did not like paying the Aztec rulers. The
conquistadors used guns and rode horses. Their
attack terrified the Aztecs, who had never seen guns
or horses before. The Spanish also carried diseases
like smallpox from Europe. These diseases weakened
and killed many Aztecs.

CHALLENGE ACTIVITY

Critical Thinking: Drawing Inferences What do you think about
Hernán Cortés and his actions toward the Aztecs? Write a one-page
opinion paper defending your point of view, giving at least three
examples to support your opinion. **HSS Analysis Skills CR 5, HI 1**

Name _____ Class _____ Date _____

The Aztec and Inca Empires

Section 2

 MAIN IDEAS

1. Aztec society was divided by social roles and by class.
2. Aztec religion required human sacrifice for keeping the gods happy.
3. The Aztecs had many achievements in science, art, and language.

 HSS 7.7

Students compare and contrast the geographic, political, economic, religious, and social structures of the Meso-American and Andean civilizations.

Key Terms and People

codex a written historical record

Section Summary

AZTEC SOCIETY

People in Aztec society had clearly defined roles and social classes that determined how they lived. Aztecs were organized into groups called *calpullis* (kahl-POO-yees), communities of families that shared land, schools, and a temple. Each *calpulli* elected a leader, and the leaders chose the king.

> **How were Aztec calpullis, or communities, organized?**
> _____
> _____

The king was the most important person in Aztec society. He lived in a great palace and had 3,000 servants to attend him. The king was in charge of law, trade and tribute, and warfare. These were huge responsibilities, but the king had people to help. These people, including tax collectors and judges, were Aztec nobles. Noble positions were passed down from fathers to sons. Young nobles went to school to learn to be government officials, military leaders, or priests.

> **Circle the number of servants who waited on the Aztec king.**

Just below the king and his nobles were priests and warriors. Priests in particular had a great influence over Aztecs' lives. Aztec warriors were highly respected for fighting to conquer new lands. They also captured victims for human sacrifice for elaborate religious rituals led by the priests.

Merchants fell just below priests and warriors. By controlling trade in the empire, they became

Interactive Reader and Study Guide

Section 2, *continued*

very rich. Most artisans were also rich and
important, particularly if they lived in the capital.

Farmers and slaves were lowest in society, though
people could sometimes improve their lives by
becoming warriors or going to a special school.
Farmers did not own their land and they were very
poor. They had to pay so much in tribute that they
often found it difficult to survive. Slaves had little to
look forward to and most were sold as laborers to
nobles or merchants. Those who were not sold were
often sacrificed to the Aztec gods.

> **What was the main reason Aztec farmers found it so difficult to survive?**
>
> _____
>
> _____
>
> _____

AZTEC RELIGION

The Aztecs believed that gods ruled all parts of life.
Their gods' powers could be seen in nature, such
as in trees or storms, and in great people, such as
in kings or ancestors. Like other Mesoamericans,
the Aztecs always tried to please their gods. They
believed sacrifice was necessary to keep the gods
happy, and that the gods literally fed on human
blood. Aztec priests led bloody ceremonies, cutting
themselves to give blood to the gods. Priests also
sacrificed nearly 10,000 human victims a year.

> **Why were Aztec religious ceremonies so bloody?**
>
> _____
>
> _____
>
> _____

SCIENCE, ART, AND LANGUAGE

The Aztecs made many scientific advances,
sometimes borrowing from the tribes they
conquered. They also studied astronomy and
created a calendar much like the Maya calendar.
The Aztecs had a rich artistic tradition and their
own writing system. They kept written history
records in a book called a **codex**. They also had a
strong oral tradition.

> **What was contained in the Aztec's codex?**
>
> _____
>
> _____

CHALLENGE ACTIVITY

Critical Thinking: Drawing Inferences If you lived in Aztec society,
what class and job would you choose? Write a one-page character study
of yourself in the Aztec world. Be creative, but also be as historically
accurate as possible. **HSS Analysis Skills CR 2, CR 4, HI 1**

The Aztec and Inca Empires

Section 3

MAIN IDEAS

1. The rise of the Inca Empire was due to conquest and the achievements of the Inca people.
2. Pizarro conquered the Incas and took control of the region.

 HSS 7.7
Students compare and contrast the geographic, political, economic, religious, and social structures of the Meso-American and Andean civilizations.

Key Terms and People

Pachacuti ruler who expanded the Inca Empire in the mid-1400s
Quechua the language of the Incas
llamas animals that are related to camels but native to South America
Atahualpa the last Incan ruler
Francisco Pizarro Spanish conquistador leader who conquered the Incas

Section Summary

THE RISE OF THE INCA EMPIRE

While the Aztecs rose in Mesoamerica, the Incas were building an empire in South America. However, the Incas were not the first civilization in South America. Around 900 BC, the first complex civilizations began to develop in what is now Peru. These included the Chavín culture in the highlands, and the Nazca, Moche, and Chimú cultures on the coast. Each of these cultures learned to adapt to its environment, made scientific advances, and developed cities. The influences of these cultures led to the development of the Inca civilization.

The Incas began as a small tribe high in the Andes. In the mid-1400s the ruler **Pachacuti** (pah-chah-KOO-tee) led the Incas to expand their territory, either through friendly agreements or by warfare. By the early 1500s, the Inca Empire stretched from northern Ecuador to central Chile.

Around 12 million people lived in the Inca Empire. To rule this huge empire, the Incas formed

> On what continent did the Incas build their empire?
> _____
> _____

> Where did the Inca tribe originate?
> _____
> _____

Interactive Reader and Study Guide

a strong central government. The Incas replaced local leaders of conquered areas with new people loyal to the Inca government. The Incas established an official language, **Quechua** (KE-chuh-wuh).

Instead of paying taxes, Incas had to "pay" their government in labor. This labor tax system was called the *mita* (MEE-tah). The government told each household what work to do. Most Incas were farmers or raised **llamas**, animals that are related to camels but native to South America. People also had to work on government-owned farms and mines, or provide grain for the army. There were no merchants or markets. Instead, government officials distributed goods collected through the *mita*.

> The Incas took children of conquered lands to the capital and trained them in Inca culture. Then they returned them to their villages to rule. Why?
> _____
> _____
> _____

> How did Incas get food, clothing and other goods?
> _____
> _____

PIZARRO CONQUERS THE INCAS

A civil war between an Inca ruler's two sons, **Atahualpa** (ah-tah-WAHL-pah) and Huáscar (WAHS-kahr), severely weakened the Inca army. Atahualpa won. On his way to be crowned king, Atahualpa heard that conquistadors led by **Francisco Pizarro** were in Peru. He agreed to meet with them. When the Spanish tried to convert Atahualpa to Christianity, he refused. The Spanish captured him and attacked the Incas, killing thousands of soldiers. The Incas brought gold and silver for Atahualpa's return, but instead the Spanish killed him. Like the Aztecs, the Incas had little chance against the weapons and diseases of the Europeans. The Spanish ruled the Inca lands for the next 300 years.

> How did the Spanish justify their first attack on the Incas?
> _____
> _____
> _____
> _____

CHALLENGE ACTIVITY

Critical Thinking: Drawing Inferences When Atahualpa met with Pizarro's men, a Spanish friar handed him a bible. The Aztec leader listened carefully. He did not hear God speak, he said, and he threw the book to the ground. The Spanish used this as a reason to attack the Incas, saying Atahualpa rejected Christianity. Write a brief essay examining Atahualpa's gesture and what he might really have meant.
HSS Analysis Skills CR 2, HI 1

Section 4

MAIN IDEAS

1. For the Incas, position in society affected daily life.

2. The Incas made great achievements in building, art, and oral literature.

 HSS 7.7
Students compare and contrast the geographic, political, economic, religious, and social structures of the Meso-American and Andean civilizations.

Key Terms and People

masonry stonework

Section Summary

SOCIETY AND DAILY LIFE

Inca society had two main social classes. The Incas from Cuzco made up the upper class. The people from conquered lands made up the lower class.

The king, priests, and government officials were upper class. Most upper-class men worked for the government. Sons of upper-class families went to school to study Quechua, religion, history, and law to prepare them for work in government. The upper-class families lived in stone houses, wore nice clothes, did not have to pay the labor tax, and often had servants. Still, as government officials, they were required to serve the people.

Most Incas belonged to the lower class. These included farmers, artisans, and servants. There were no slaves in Inca society. The work was done by lower-class men and women to pay the labor tax. Most children worked and did not go to school. But some carefully chosen young girls were trained in weaving, cooking, and religion. Then they were sent to serve the king or work in the temples. Lower-class Incas lived outside Cuzco in small houses. By law they had to wear plain clothes. Also, they could not own more goods than they needed.

The Incas had an official religion, which they taught to conquered people. Inca religion was based

In what city did upper-class Incas live?

_____

_____

Who worked hardest in Inca Society?

_____

_____

Section 4, *continued*

on the belief that Inca rulers were related to the sun god. People thought their rulers never really died. Inca religious ceremonies often included sacrifice. But unlike the Maya and the Aztecs, the Incas rarely sacrificed humans. They usually killed a llama or offered cloth and food to their gods. The Incas also believed certain mountaintops, rocks, and springs had magical powers, and they performed sacrifices there as well.

> **Incas believed their rulers were related to whom?**
> _____
> _____

BUILDING, ART, AND ORAL LITERATURE

Inca work was of high quality. They are known in particular for their **masonry,** or stonework. They built massive buildings and forts of huge stone blocks. Workers cut the blocks so precisely that they did not need cement to hold the blocks together. Even today it is nearly impossible to fit a knife blade between the stones. In fact, many Inca buildings in Cuzco are still being used. The Incas also built a good system of roads in their empire.

> **The Incas excelled in the use of what building material?**
> _____
> _____

Artisans did beautiful metalwork. They even created a life-size field of corn made of gold and silver in a temple courtyard. Incas also made some of the best textiles. Archaeologists have found brightly colored Inca fabrics still in excellent condition.

Unlike the Maya and the Aztecs, the Incas had no written language. Instead, Incas passed down stories and songs orally. Official "memorizers" learned long poems about Inca legends and history. After the conquistadors came, some Incas learned Spanish and wrote about Inca legends.

> **Underline the colorful phrase describing the official Inca historians.**

CHALLENGE ACTIVITY

Critical Thinking: Drawing Inferences Unlike many societies, the Inca used labor as a form of currency, rather than money or a trading market. What are the advantages of this type of economic system, and what are the disadvantages? Write a brief essay explaining your answer. **HSS Analysis Skills CS1, HI 6**

The Age of Exploration

HISTORY–SOCIAL SCIENCE STANDARDS
HSS 7.11 Students analyze political and economic change in the sixteenth, seventeenth, and eighteenth centuries (the Age of Exploration, the Enlightenment, and the Age of Reason).
HSS Analysis Skills HI 1 Explain central issues and problems from the past.

CHAPTER SUMMARY

Plant and animal exchanges	led to	**development of mining and plantations in the Americas**
Mercantilism and triangular trade	led to	**exploitation of Africans and Indians**
European cottage industries	led to	**increased wealth among individuals**
Demand for manufactured goods	led to	**birth of capitalism**

COMPREHENSION AND CRITICAL THINKING

Use information from the graphic organizer to answer the following questions.

1. **Explain** Who ran the plantations and mining industries that developed in the Americas?

_____

2. **Identify Cause and Effect** Why did Europeans prohibit trading between the different American colonies founded by different countries?

_____

_____

3. **Evaluate** Who benefited from the development of capitalism?

_____

_____

4. **Draw a Conclusion** Who suffered from the development of capitalism?

_____

_____

The Age of Exploration

MAIN IDEAS

1. Europeans had a desire and opportunity to explore.
2. Portuguese and Spanish explorations led to discoveries of new trade routes, lands, and people.
3. English and French explorers found land in North America.
4. A new European worldview developed because of the discoveries.

 HSS 7.11
Students analyze political and economic change in the sixteenth, seventeenth, and eighteenth centuries (the Age of Exploration, the Enlightenment, and the Age of Reason).

Key Terms and People

Henry the Navigator Portuguese prince who started a sailing school and funded many expeditions

Vasco da Gama first explorer to sail safely around Africa to India

Christopher Columbus Italian explorer who accidentally discovered the Americas

Ferdinand Magellan Portuguese navigator who first circumnavigated the globe

circumnavigate to go all the way around

Francis Drake famous English pirate who robbed Spanish ships in the Americas

Spanish Armada huge fleet of Spanish ships defeated during an attack on England in 1588

Section Summary

DESIRE AND OPPORTUNITY TO EXPLORE

Improvements in navigational tools, cartography, and shipbuilding spurred an interest in discovery and exploration in Europe during the 1400s. Explorers set off in search of new trade routes to Asia to find rare spices, to spread Christianity, and to discover new lands and people.

> **List four motivations that drove European explorers during the 1400s and 1500s.**
>
> _____
> _____
> _____
> _____
> _____

PORTUGUESE AND SPANISH EXPLORATIONS

Henry the Navigator was an influential early figure in Portuguese exploration. Henry built an observatory and navigation school for sailors, and funded many sailing expeditions. With Henry's

> **Henry the Navigator never left Portugal. Why was he so influential in early Portuguese explorations?**
>
> _____
> _____
> _____

Section 1, continued

help, a sailor named **Vasco da Gama** became the first person to sail safely around Africa to India.

Christopher Columbus was Italian but he offered his services to Spain. Knowing the world was round, he set out to reach Asia by heading west. His voyage led to the accidental discovery of the Americas. It was **Ferdinand Magellan**, a Portuguese navigator sailing for Spain, who first **circumnavigated** the globe, although he was killed before the end of the journey. Following Columbus's lead, the Spanish conquistadors sailed to the Americas in the early 1500s and conquered the Inca and Aztec civilizations.

> **Why did Columbus think he was sailing to Asia?**
> _____
> _____
> _____

ENGLISH AND FRENCH IN AMERICA

As Portugal and Spain secured southern trade routes, France and England went north. Early journeys by explorers from both countries again confused North America with Asia, but they secured claims to the land. The famous pirate **Francis Drake**, in the service of England, raided Spanish ships for their treasures. Spain retaliated by sending a fleet of ships, the **Spanish Armada**, to attack England in 1588. The English navy defeated the Armada with the help of a great storm at sea. Spanish sea power never recovered.

> **How did English pirate Francis Drake contribute to Spain's loss of control over the sea?**
> _____
> _____
> _____

A NEW EUROPEAN WORLD VIEW

After the voyages of the 1400s and 1500s, Europeans saw new and more accurate maps that showed the entire world. This ushered in a new period of European influence in the world.

CHALLENGE ACTIVITY

Critical Thinking: Drawing Inferences European explorers had to spend as much time raising money as they did sailing. Pretend that you are an explorer living in Spain, Portugal, France, or England during the 1400s. You need to convince a rich patron to pay for a sailing expedition. Write an argument in which you lay out the reasons and purpose for your trip. **HSS Analysis Skills CS 3, HI 5, HI 6**

The Age of Exploration

MAIN IDEAS

1. Plants and animals were exchanged among Europe, Asia, Africa, and the Americas.

2. Culture and technology changed as ideas were exchanged between Europe and the Americas.

3. Society and the economy changed in Europe and the Americas.

 HSS 7.11
Students analyze political and economic change in the sixteenth, seventeenth, and eighteenth centuries (the Age of Exploration, the Enlightenment, and the Age of Reason).

Key Terms and People

Columbian Exchange exchange of plants, animals and ideas between the New World (the Americas) and the Old World (Europe)

plantations large farms

Bartolomé de las Casas Spanish priest who opposed harsh treatment of the Indians, and proposed bringing slaves from Africa to work the plantations

racism belief that some people are better than others because of racial traits

Section Summary

PLANTS AND ANIMALS

One major impact on the world due to the European sea explorations was the exchange of plants, animals, and ideas between the New World (the Americas) and the Old World (Europe). This is called the **Columbian Exchange**.

Europeans brought crops such as bananas and sugarcane from Asia to Central and South America. They also planted oranges, onions, and lettuce. Cows, goats, sheep, horses, pigs, and chickens were also brought to the New World. Europeans took home tomatoes, potatoes, beans, squash, avocados, pineapples, tobacco, and chili peppers. This exchange changed the world's eating habits, not just in Europe and the Americas. Items like sweet potatoes and peanuts became popular in Africa. In China, peanuts and maize became major crops.

> Underline the names of the main crops that criss-crossed oceans in the Columbian Exchange.

> What was new about the animals Europeans introduced to the Americas?
>
> _____
> _____

CULTURE AND TECHNOLOGY

Besides food and animals, religion and language
were probably the biggest changes Europeans
introduced to the New World. Both Protestant and
Catholic missionaries traveled to the Americas to
convert people to Christianity. Missionaries set up
schools to teach European languages. In some
places, Christianity blended with local customs to
create new religious practices.

> Underline the phrase that expresses the main goal of missionaries who traveled to the New World.

The Europeans introduced technologies and
animals that made life and work easier, such as
horses for transportation and the oxen and plough
for farming. They also brought guns, steel, and the
wheel. New industries developed from these
innovations, such as **plantations** and mining,
run mostly by the Europeans.

> What two factors enabled plantations and mining to begin in the Americas?
> _____
> _____
> _____

SOCIETY AND THE ECONOMY

Sugarcane plantations and mines made a lot
of money for Spain and Portugal. But these
plantations were built on the backs of American
Indians, who were forced into slave labor to work
in these industries. Many Native Americans died as
a result of harsh treatment and new diseases.

Not everyone agreed with the European policy.
Spanish priest **Bartolomé de las Casas** was
particularly critical of the treatment of the Indians.
Unfortunately, las Casas' solution to the problem
was to use Africans as slaves instead of American
Indians. This created a new society based on
racism. The white Europeans considered
themselves superior to the darker-skinned
Indians and Africans, and those of mixed blood.

> What did Bartolomé de las Casas propose to stop the slave labor and mistreatment of American Indians?
> _____
> _____
> _____
> _____

CHALLENGE ACTIVITY

Critical Thinking: Drawing Inferences The roots of modern American
cultures were built on the backs of African and American Indian slaves,
who were treated as lesser people because of the color of their skin. In
what ways does this racism still permeate the United States today? **HSS
Analysis Skills CR 4, HI 2**

The Age of Exploration

Section 3

MAIN IDEAS

1. A new economic system called mercantilism emerged.

2. New trading patterns developed between the 1600s and 1700s.

3. Power in Europe shifted as a result of new trade routes, banking, and increased manufacturing.

4. Market economies changed business in Europe.

 HSS 7.11

Students analyze political and economic change in the sixteenth, seventeenth, and eighteenth centuries (the Age of Exploration, the Enlightenment, and the Age of Reason).

Key Terms and People

mercantilism trading system in which the government controls all economic activity

balance of trade relationship between imported goods and exported goods

cottage industry home-based manufacturing business run by families

atlas collection of maps

capitalism system in which individuals and private businesses run most industries

market economy system in which individuals decide what goods and services to buy

Section Summary

A NEW ECONOMY

Europeans saw the American colonies as a way to get rich. An economic system called **mercantilism** came into being. In mercantilism the government controls all economic activity in a country and its colonies. This makes the government stronger and richer. Mercantilism was the main economic policy in Europe between 1500 and 1800.

To stay rich each country tried to maintain a **balance of trade** by exporting more goods than they imported. Colonies of competing countries could not trade with one another. Each colony traded only with its home country. Colonies served as both sources of raw materials and places to sell finished manufactured products. These products were made by an increasing number of

> How does a balance of trade benefit a country?
>
> _____
>
> _____
>
> _____

Name _____ Class _____ Date _____

Section 3, *continued*

European-based **cottage industries**, small home-based businesses run by families.

> Underline the definition of cottage industries.

NEW TRADING PATTERNS

A vast trading network among Europe, Africa, and the Americas called triangular trade began. Raw materials, manufactured products, and slaves were exchanged. The Portuguese, English, and Dutch increased the new Atlantic slave trade, cramming Africans into ships without food or water.

> Why do you think the trading network among Europe, Africa, and the Americas was called triangular trade?
> _____
> _____
> _____

POWER SHIFTS IN EUROPE

Mercantilism was most successful in Portugul and Spain, but the English and French discovered new northern trade routes and established a banking system that helped shift economic power in their favor. A new book of highly improved maps, called an **atlas**, helped improve northern trading expeditions. The Dutch, meanwhile, formed the first company designed to deal directly with trade from Africa and Asia, which helped them control many trading posts there.

> Why do you think an atlas was helpful to traders?
> _____
> _____
> _____

MARKET ECONOMIES

Increased wealth in Europe led to an increased demand for manufactured goods. People who came up with ways to increase the supply to meet the demand for goods created the basis of **capitalism**, a new economic system in which individuals and private business controlled most industries. This stimulates competition among manufacturers and creates a **market economy**, in which individuals decide what goods and services they want to buy.

> What stimulates competition in a capitalist economic system?
> _____
> _____
> _____
> _____

CHALLENGE ACTIVITY

Critical Thinking: Drawing Inferences You are a shoemaker in England during the 1700s. You hear that the American colonies are in desperate need of shoes. A trader asks you if you can fill an order for 5,000 pairs of shoes—by next week! You say yes. What will you do to fill the order?
HSS Analysis Skills HI 1, HI 3

Enlightenment and Revolution

HISTORY–SOCIAL SCIENCE STANDARDS
HSS 7.11 Students analyze political and economic change in the sixteenth, seventeenth, and eighteenth centuries (the Age of Exploration, the Enlightenment, and the Age of Reason).
HSS Analysis Skill HR5 Students detect the different historical points of view on historical events and determine the context in which the historical statements were made (the questions asked, sources used, author's perspectives).

CHAPTER SUMMARY

Event	Key People	Key Ideas
Enlightenment	Locke, _____, Rousseau	
American Revolution	Jefferson,	
French Revolution	King Louis XVI	

COMPREHENSION AND CRITICAL THINKING

Use the answers to the following questions to fill in the graphic organizer above.

1. Explain Which country was the first to abolish the divine right of kings?

_____

2. Identify Cause and Effect Why were the American colonists unhappy with British rule?

_____

3. Evaluate Why do you think the French took longer to form a democracy than England or America?

_____

4. Draw a Conclusion What key ideas from the Enlightenment became founding principles in the English, American, and French declarations of human rights?

_____

_____

Enlightenment and Revolution

MAIN IDEAS

1. The Enlightenment was also called the Age of Reason.
2. The Enlightenment's roots can be traced back to earlier ideas.
3. New ideas came mainly from French and British thinkers.

 HSS 7.11

Students analyze political and economic change in the sixteenth, seventeenth, and eighteenth centuries (the Age of Exploration, the Enlightenment, and the Age of Reason).

Key Terms and People

Enlightenment period in which people valued the use of reason as a guide to improving society

secular non-religious

Voltaire French writer who mocked government and religion

salon social gathering in which people discuss ideas

Mary Wollstonecraft British writer who championed women's rights

Section Summary

THE AGE OF REASON

The Scientific Revolution and the European exploration of the Americas caused a growing number of European scholars to challenge long-held beliefs about science, religion, and government. They believed the newly developed power of human reason could be used to increase knowledge, freedom, and happiness in the world. This use of reason to define politics and society defined a period called the **Enlightenment**.

> What do you think was "enlightened" about the Enlightenment?
> _____
> _____
> _____
> _____

THE ENLIGHTENMENT'S ROOTS

Enlightenment thinkers were influenced by the ideas of the ancient Greeks and Romans, the Christian Reformation, the Renaissance, and the Scientific Revolution. Greek philosophers like Aristotle believed there was a natural order to the world. This had been further expanded into the

> Underline the sentence that indicates how Aristotle inspired Enlightenment thinkers.

Interactive Reader and Study Guide

natural law envisioned by the Romans. Thomas
Aquinas's demonstration that faith could be
paired with reason caused people to challenge
the church's authority. Renaissance thinkers had
shifted emphasis from God to individual human
achievement.

> **What institution had its authority undermined by the Enlightenment?**
> _____
> _____

Reformers like Martin Luther and scientists like
Galileo had challenged the church's understanding
of events. They found that church teaching was not
always in line with reality or logic. All this led to a
more **secular**, or non-religious, view of how society
could be ordered.

> **Why did the Enlightenment cause a more secular movement?**
> _____
> _____

NEW IDEAS

French philosophers like **Voltaire** (vohl-TAYR)
were openly outspoken in their disregard for the
authority of the church and existing governments.
He mocked both government and religion freely in
his writings. He got in trouble for this, of course,
and so spoke passionately against censorship.

Another Frenchman, Denis Diderot (dee-DROH),
edited the first book to collect these ideas, a
multivolume work called the *Encyclopedia*. It was
banned by the king of France and the pope. People
began to sponsor **salons**, social gatherings to
discuss ideas.

Though women were still not considered equal
to men, many women sponsored salons. British
writer **Mary Wollstonecraft** argued in favor of
women's rights.

> **In what country did the subject of women's rights first surface as a serious idea?**
> _____
> _____

CHALLENGE ACTIVITY

Critical Thinking: Drawing Inferences If you were to hold a salon today,
what would the topics of discussion include? Have students in the
classroom define important topics (e.g. war, racism, politics, poverty,
teen pregnancy, etc.) and discuss ideas on how to resolve these issues.
Remind your students that all ideas are equally valid, but students must
defend their opinions with reasons, and be prepared for possible
disagreement. **HSS Analysis Skills CS 1, CR 2, CR 3**

Enlightenment and Revolution

MAIN IDEAS
1. The Enlightenment influenced some monarchies.
2. Enlightenment thinkers helped the growth of democratic ideas.
3. In America, the Enlightenment inspired a struggle for independence.

 HSS 7.11
Students analyze political and economic change in the sixteenth, seventeenth, and eighteenth centuries (the Age of Exploration, the Enlightenment, and the Age of Reason).

Key Terms and People

John Locke English philosopher who said government is a contract between ruler and the people

natural rights Locke's idea that every person has the right to life, liberty, and property

Charles-Louis Montesquieu French philosopher who said government should be divided into separate branches, each branch limiting the power of the other branch

Jean-Jacques Rousseau French writer who proposed the idea of popular sovereignty

popular sovereignty government that expresses the will of the people

Benjamin Franklin American philosopher, scientiest, and statesman who argued before the British Parliment for the repeal of extra taxes on colonists

Thomas Jefferson American statesman who proposed the idea of colonial independence

Academic Vocabulary

contract a binding legal agreement

Section Summary

ENLIGHTENMENT INFLUENCE ON MONARCHIES

In the 1600s most European monarchs thought they ruled by right imparted directly from God. The Enlightenment challenged this belief. It inspired some rulers to try to improve life for common people. These rulers were called enlightened despots. Although the enlightened despots made some improvements in their countires, many Enlightenment thinkers, began to consider the need for democracy.

> **Look up the word "despot" in a dictionary and write the definition here:**
> _____
> _____
> _____
> _____

Interactive Reader and Study Guide

Name _____ Class _____ Date _____

Section 2, *continued*

DEMOCRATIC IDEAS

Three Enlightenment thinkers set the stage for modern democracy. English philosopher **John Locke** argued against a ruler's divine right, proposing instead that government should be based on a **contract** between the ruler and the people. He also said the government should have one goal: the peace, safety, and public good of the people. Locke said people had **natural rights** to life, liberty, and property.

> What did John Locke believe was the only goal of a government?
> _____
> _____
> _____

French thinker **Charles-Louis Montesquieu** (mohn-te-SKYOO) expanded on these ideas, saying that government should be divided into separate branches, each one limiting the power of the other. Another Frenchman, **Jean-Jacques Rousseau** (roo-SOH), proposed the idea of **popular sovereignty**, that governments express the will of the people.

> Underline Rousseau and Montesquieu's ideas about government.

THE ENLIGHTENMENT IN AMERICA

British colonists living in America were deeply moved by these ideas. When the British government began to chip away at what the colonists saw as their rights, they began to protest. They began by arguing against the extra taxes Britain imposed on colonists for certain products. American printer and scientist **Benjamin Franklin** traveled to London and argued successfully in Parliament for the repeal of these taxes. Franklin argued that the British government had no right to tax the colonists because the colonists had no representative in Parliment. Meanwhile, **Thomas Jefferson**, a scholar, scientist, and farmer, proposed the idea of independence for the colonies.

> Who were the two American colonists who took conscious action based on the ideas of Locke, Montesquieu, and Rousseau?
> _____
> _____
> _____

CHALLENGE ACTIVITY

Critical Thinking: Drawing Inferences Write up your own legal contract with your teacher about how to preserve the peace, safety, and public good in your classroom. Be very specific and thoughtful about the rules you choose. Remember, both sides need to follow rules. **HSS Analysis Skills CR 2, HI 1**

Interactive Reader and Study Guide

Enlightenment and Revolution

MAIN IDEAS
1. Revolution and reform changed the government of England.
2. Enlightenment ideas led to democracy in America.
3. The French Revolution caused major changes in France's government.

 HSS 7.11
Students analyze political and economic change in the sixteenth, seventeenth, and eighteenth centuries (the Age of Exploration, the Enlightenment, and the Age of Reason).

Key Terms and People

English Bill of Rights document that listed rights agreed on between British rulers, the Parliament, and the people in 1689

Declaration of Independence document declaring the colonie's independence form British rule in 1776

regime government in power

Declaration of the Rights of Man and of the Citizen document granting freedom of speech, the press, and religion for the French

Academic Vocabulary

ideals ideas or goals that people try to live up to

Section Summary

REVOLUTION AND REFORM IN ENGLAND

In England, the uneasy relationship been Parliament and the monarchy exploded into a civil war in 1642. A series of rulers took power before Parliament invited William of Orange to invade and overthrow the king in 1688. William took power, but only after agreeing to sign an **English Bill of Rights** for Parliament and the English people in 1689. William became king, but shared power with Parliment.

> **When was the English Bill of Rights signed?**
> _____
> _____

DEMOCRACY IN AMERICA

The English Bill of Rights did not apply to the American colonies. The colonies developed their own governing bodies, but were still subject to burdensome taxes and trade restrictions. Though

> **Underline the phrase that indicates the main American grievances against English rule.**

Interactive Reader and Study Guide

Section 3, *continued*

not all Americans wanted independence, everyone wanted more equitable treatment. When their protests were put down by British troops, the colonists organized militias to protect themselves. In 1776 Thomas Jefferson drafted the **Declaration of Independence**, announcing the colonies' independence from British rule.

> **What general area of European thought underlay the push for independence in America??**
> _____
> _____

The Declaration clearly expresses Enlightenment **ideals**. Britain eventually gave up the fight and recognized the independence of the colonies. A new government plan for the United States, in keeping with Montesquieu's idea about separate branches, was developed by James Madison and others.

> **Circle the name of the person who drafted a new form of government for the United States of America.**

THE FRENCH REVOLUTION

The American Revolution inspired the French to rebel against their own **regime**. Most commoners in France had no say in government at all, paying high taxes with virtually no rights. A National Assembly was formed to demand rights from King Louis XVI, but he refused to listen.

> **Why were the commoners of France so outraged at the king?**
> _____
> _____
> _____

The French Revolution began in 1789. The king eventually agreed to rules similar to the English Bill of Rights and the American Declaration of Independence, called the **Declaration of the Rights of Man and the Citizen**. Still, Louis was eventually tried and executed. It took the French several years to develop a stable new government because the rage of the commoners, called the Reign of Terror, was hard to control. Eventually, France also installed a democratic system of government.

> **How did Louis XVI die?**
> _____
> _____

CHALLENGE ACTIVITY

Critical Thinking: Drawing Inferences You are a revolutionary agitator, either in England, the British colonies in America, or in France. How would you inspire your neighbors and friends to join you in the fight? Develop a character and write a persuasive speech that is historically appropriate to the period. Depending on the country you choose, remember to mention the other country's revolutions whose ideas inspired your own. **HSS Analysis Skills CR 2, HI 1**